MADE WITH LOVE

MADE WITH LOVE

50 beautiful, sweet gifts for friends and family

Aimee Twigger

GIBBS SMITH
TO ENRICH AND INSPIRE HUMANKIND

CONTENTS

3. Cookies and confectionery

4. Party treats

Acknowledgments and Index 190

A NOTE FROM AIMEE

For as long I can remember I have been creative, and when I found my love for baking a couple of years ago, the two seemed to naturally merge together. As the theme of this book tells you, creating sweet things is what I love to do most – I have always had a sweet tooth. And the treat should not only taste sweet, it should look sweet as well. When I bake I want to create a work of art; I always imagine how the finished product might look before I even start to think about the recipe.

I enjoy styling my treats as much as I do baking them. I don't have fancy equipment – just a standard camera and loads of wonderful props and baking tools. I've included a list of equipment stockists at the back of the book; however, I often search in local thrift stores and on eBay for props and vintage baking equipment. I love these vintage pieces because I always imagine they have a story behind them, and they look great in photos.

Thrift stores are great places even when you're not styling your food for a photograph. Vintage tins and boxes make great gifts, especially when they're filled with beautiful treats. All of the recipes in this book work perfectly as edible gifts that you can share with loved ones and friends. The recipes are also easy to make, but if you're unsure I've included difficulty ratings (with ⁄ for easy and ⁄ ⁄ ⁄ for difficult) as well as step-by-step photos to help you along with the trickier bits.

Love, Aimee x

BAKER'S NOTES

Ingredients

Butter: I always use butter at room temperature for cakes and chilled, cubed butter for pastry or cookies.

Eggs: When baking cakes or cupcakes, make sure your eggs are at room temperature.

Baking powder: To check if your baking powder is still active add a spoonful into some water. If it fizzes up, it's still good to use.

Flour: There are so many different types of flour with different gluten levels, such as all-purpose flour, self-rising flour, spelt flour and rye flour. I tend to use plain or self-rising flour for most of my recipes but I like to use spelt flour, too – it is thought of as an ancient grain. Sieve the flour to help prevent any lumps in a batter. When making a cake, always fold in the flour rather than mix it with a hand-held electric beater. When flour is folded in, it doesn't build up as much gluten, which helps to make the cake light and fluffy.

Equipment

Food processor: I swear by my food processor and recommend that you get one. I use it for so many things, from making cookie dough and pastry to puréeing fruit and chopping up ingredients – I just love it. You don't need to waste money on an expensive one with loads of attachments. Mine is just a cheap one, and I never use any of the attachments except the cutting blade. I've noted in the recipes when a food processor is required.

Stand mixer: Another kitchen gadget I would recommend is a stand mixer; it is very handy when making meringues or marshmallows. I've noted in the recipes when a stand mixer is required.

Rubber spatula: This is my favourite kitchen tool. I use it for most of my baking because it's so versatile. Spatulas are great for folding in mixtures, and they scrape the sides of a bowl very well so everything is mixed properly and there is no waste. A spatula can also be used to spread icing over cakes and cupcakes.

1. Cupcakes

Little honey cakes with figs, pistachios and mascarpone

Makes 6 cakes   Difficulty rating 🥄

For the cakes
4¹/₂ oz/9 tablespoons butter

¹/₂ cup superfine sugar

2 eggs

2 tablespoons honey, plus extra
  for drizzling

3³/₄ oz/³/₄ cup self-rising flour

2 tablespoons crushed pistachio
  kernels, plus extra for
  sprinkling

For the icing and topping
8 oz/1 cup mascarpone cheese

1 cup confectioners' sugar

3 figs

Equipment
Silicone cupcake mold

Prep time: 10 minutes

Baking time: 12 minutes

Decorating time: 15 minutes

For the cakes
Preheat the oven to 350°F.

Cream the butter and sugar together in a bowl until pale and creamy. Beat in the eggs one at a time, making sure that each one is properly combined before adding the next. Add 2 tablespoons honey and mix through. Sift in the flour, add 2 tablespoons of pistachios and fold into the mixture.

Spoon the batter into the cake mold, filling the mold about three-quarters full. Bake for 12 minutes and then allow to cool.

For the icing and topping
Mix the mascarpone with the confectioners' sugar. Slice any risen tops off the cakes and sandwich two of the small cakes together with the mascarpone mixture. Drizzle on a little of the honey. Add some more mascarpone mixture on top, drizzle on some honey and then sprinkle with crushed pistachios. Top each cake with half a fig.

EDIBLE ROSE CAKE POPS

I had the idea one day to create an edible bouquet.
These roses are in fact cake pops with fondant petals.
I used stems from faux flowers instead of lollipop sticks
to make them appear more realistic.

This would be great for Mother's Day.

Edible rose cake pops

Makes 20 cake pops   *Difficulty rating* 🥄🥄🥄

For the cake balls
4 ¹/₂ oz /9 tablespoons butter
¹/₂ cup superfine sugar
2 eggs
¹/₂ teaspoon vanilla bean paste
3 ³/₄ oz/³/₄ cup self-rising flour
¹/₄ teaspoon salt

For the petals
Pink food coloring
9 oz package of fondant or
   modeling chocolate

Equipment
Cake pop mold
Faux flower stems or
   lollipop sticks
Rolling pin

Prep time: 10 minutes
Baking time: 11–15 minutes
Decorating time: 15 minutes per cake pop

For the cake balls
Preheat the oven to 350°F.

Cream the butter and sugar together in a bowl until pale and creamy. Beat in the eggs one at a time, then stir in the vanilla bean paste. Sift in the flour and salt and fold into the mixture.

Spoon the batter into a cake pop mold, filling the mold to the top. Put the lid on the mold, bake for 11–15 minutes and then allow to cool.

When completely cool, insert faux flower stems or lollipop sticks into the cake balls.

For the petals
Knead a little food coloring into the fondant or modeling chocolate, adding a small amount at a time until you achieve the desired color. Take a small ball of fondant and roll it out into a petal shape. Wrap the petal around one of the cake balls, pinching it together at the top (see figure 1). Add a second petal slightly overlapping the first. To stick the petals together, brush the back of each petal with a little water.

Continue adding petals around the cake ball until it is completely covered (see figure 2). Add a second layer of petals, curving the top edges outwards slightly (see figure 3). Add a third layer of petals, but curve out the top edges even more (see figure 4).

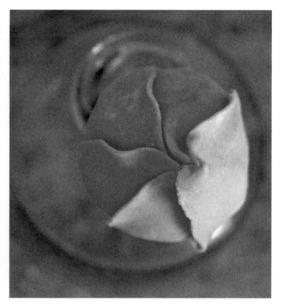

1. Place the petal onto the cake ball and pinch at the top

2. Overlap the petals and stick them together by brushing the back of each petal with a little water

3. Add a second layer of petals in a circle, gradually opening out the top edges

4. On the outer layer of the rose, open the petals out even more

SUCCULENT CUPCAKES

I'm so happy with how these cakes turned out. I enjoy creating things that make people do a double-take and think "Is that real?" These cakes have a chocolate sponge base and chocolate icing and are decorated with a crushed biscuit and brown sugar "sand" topped with fondant "succulents."

Echevua Setosa
Van demuuta

ROUDABUSH'S SEED STO
CORNER FRONT & DOCK STS.

Succulent cupcakes

Makes 6 cupcakes   *Difficulty rating* ✎ ✎

For the sponge cake
4¹/2 oz/9 tablespoons butter
¹/2 cup superfine sugar
2 eggs
¹/2 teaspoon vanilla extract
3³/4 oz/³/4 cup all-purpose flour
1 teaspoon baking powder
1¹/2 tablespoons unsweetened
    cocoa powder
3 teaspoons milk

For the buttercream
4¹/2 oz/9 tablespoons butter
1¹/4 cups confectioners' sugar
2 tablespoons unsweetened
    cocoa powder

To decorate
3 graham crackers or equivalent
    amount of vanilla wafers
¹/4 cup brown sugar, firmly
    packed
9 oz package of green fondant
Deep purple edible lustre dust
6 plant markers

Equipment
6 small peat pots
Flower cutters in two sizes
Ball tool
Scissors

Prep time: 10 minutes
Baking time: 15–20 minutes
Decorating time: 30 minutes

For the sponge cake
Preheat the oven to 350°F. Line six small peat pots with baking paper. To make the sponge, cream the butter and sugar together in a bowl until pale and creamy. Beat in the eggs one at a time, then stir in the vanilla extract. Sift in the flour, baking powder and cocoa and fold into the mixture. Stir in the milk. Spoon some cake batter into each pot until about three-quarters full, bake for 15–20 minutes and then allow to cool.

For the buttercream
Mix the buttercream ingredients together until smooth. Slice the top off each cake and trim down the baking paper so that it's not visible. Spread some buttercream onto the top of each cake (see figure 1).

To decorate
To make the sand, crush the biscuits and mix with the sugar. Sprinkle some sand on top of each cake (see figure 1).

To make the succulents, roll out the fondant. Using flower cutters in two sizes, cut two large and three small flowers (I used hydrangea-shaped cutters). Use a ball tool to curve each leaf (see figure 2) and then layer the smaller flowers on top of the larger ones, sticking them together using a brush and some water. For the center of each succulent, roll a small cone of fondant (see figure 3) and snip into it with scissors to make it look like a tight bud of leaves. Brush lustre dust lightly onto the edges of each leaf. Place them into egg cups to help keep their shape and allow to harden. Put a succulent on top of each cupcake (see figure 4).

1. Spread buttercream on top of each cake and sprinkle with biscuit sand

2. Curve each cut leaf with a ball tool

3. Roll a small cone of fondant and place in the center

4. Brush the leaves with lustre dust. Stick a plant marker in each

Lavender cupcakes with edible flowers

Makes 24 cupcakes   Difficulty rating 🖌

For the candied flowers
Selection of edible flowers, such
    as primroses and violets
1/4 cup sugar
2 oz egg whites (about
    1 egg white)

For the cupcakes
9 oz/18 tablespoons butter
1²/₃ cups superfine sugar
4 eggs
13 oz/2¹/₂ cups all-purpose flour
2¹/₂ teaspoons baking powder
1 teaspoon salt
1 cup milk
1 teaspoon lavender extract

For the icing
1/2 cup confectioners' sugar
1¹/₂ tablespoons lemon juice
Lilac food coloring

Equipment
Small paintbrush
Cooling rack
Cupcake tin
24 cupcake cases

Prep time: flowers: 10 minutes, plus overnight to harden;
cakes: 10 minutes
Baking time: 15–20 minutes
Decorating time: 10 minutes

For the candied flowers
Wash the flowers and dry them gently. Place the superfine sugar
in a small dish. Using a small paintbrush, paint some egg white
onto each flower and then dip the flower into the superfine
sugar. Place on a wire cooling rack and leave overnight to
harden.

For the cupcakes
The following day, preheat the oven to 350°F.

Cream the butter and sugar together in a bowl until pale and
creamy. Beat in the eggs one at a time. Sift in the flour, baking
powder and salt and fold into the mixture. Add the milk and
lavender extract and mix until the cake batter is smooth.

Spoon into the cake cases, about three-quarters full, and bake for
15–20 minutes. Allow to cool.

For the icing
Mix the confectioners' sugar and lemon juice with 1–2 teaspoons
of cold water. Stir in some food coloring, adding a small amount
at a time until you achieve a color you like. Cover the cupcakes
with icing, then gently press some candied flowers on top.

RASPBERRY AND WHITE CHOCOLATE MUFFINS

I decided to pipe a flower on top of each muffin to make them look pretty enough for Mother's Day. It's really easy to do – trust me, I am awful at piping! I added raspberries and white chocolate to the cake mixture and used cream cheese icing for the flowers, which turned out looking a little like carnations.

Raspberry and white chocolate muffins

Makes 24 muffins   Difficulty rating 𝓟 𝓟 𝓟

For the muffins
9 oz/18 tablespoons butter
1²/₃ cups superfine sugar
4 eggs
1 cup milk
13 oz/2¹/₂ cups all-purpose flour
2¹/₂ teaspoons baking powder
1 teaspoon salt
1 cup raspberries
¹/₃ cup chopped white chocolate

For the icing
³/₄ cup whipping cream
¹/₂ cup confectioners' sugar
1 teaspoon vanilla extract
12 oz/1¹/₂ cups cream cheese
Pink food coloring

Equipment
Cupcake tin
24 cupcake cases
Piping bag
Petal nozzle

Prep time: 10 minutes
Baking time: 25 minutes
Decorating time: 10 minutes per cake

For the muffins
Preheat the oven to 350°F.

Cream the butter and sugar together in a bowl until pale and creamy. Beat in the eggs one at a time, then add the milk. Sift in the flour, baking powder and salt and fold into the mixture. Add half the raspberries and gently mix in, crushing the raspberries a little. Stir in the remaining raspberries and the white chocolate.

Spoon the mixture into the cupcake cases, about three-quarters full, bake for 25 minutes and then allow to cool.

For the icing
Whip the cream, confectioners' sugar and vanilla extract together until stiff peaks form. Add the cream cheese and a small amount of pink coloring and mix until well combined. Put 1 tablespoon of icing onto each muffin and smooth it out to cover each cake completely (see figure 1).

Put the remaining icing into the piping bag with the petal nozzle. With the widest part of the nozzle nearest to the cake (see figure 2), pipe a circle to form the center of the flower. Pipe another layer of icing around the center. Start piping petals by touching the nozzle to the cake and then bringing the piping bag up and making a semi-circle (see figure 3).

Continue piping larger petals, flicking out your wrist slightly the further out you get (see figure 4). Keep adding petals until the whole muffin is covered.

1. Smooth a tablespoon of icing on each muffin

2. With the widest part of the petal nozzle nearest the cake, pipe a circle to form the center of the flower

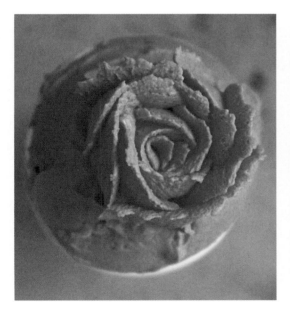

3. Continue outwards from the center, piping larger and larger semi-circles

4. As you reach the edge of the muffin, flick your wrist out so that the petals on the outside appear more open

MINI SPELT CAKES

I bought a mini muffin tin one weekend and found some tiny paper cases to fit in it (I think they were meant for truffles). I like anything that's miniature — I don't really know why, but I think it's the novelty factor of it. I was so excited to make these bite-sized cupcakes.

1. Use a paintbrush to paint some egg white onto each flower

2. Dip the flower in superfine sugar

3. The cakes are ready when you touch them lightly and they bounce back

4. Pipe icing onto each cake and place a candied flower on top

Mini spelt cakes

Makes 12 cakes   Difficulty rating

For the candied flowers
Selection of edible flowers
    and petals, such as violets,
    primroses, tulip petals
    and rosebuds
1/4 cup superfine sugar
1 egg white

For the cupcakes
2¹/4 oz/4¹/4 tablespoons butter
1/4 cup superfine sugar
1 egg
1/2 teaspoon rose water
2¹/4 oz/1/2 cup spelt flour
1/4 teaspoon baking powder
3 teaspoons milk

For the icing
2 oz/1/4 cup cream cheese
1/2 cup confectioners' sugar
Pink or purple food coloring

Equipment
Small paintbrush
Cooling rack
Mini muffin tin
12 mini cake cases
Piping bag

Prep time: flowers: 10 minutes, plus overnight to harden;
cakes: 10 minutes
Baking time: 8–10 minutes
Decorating time: 10 minutes

For the candied flowers
Wash the flowers and dry them gently. Place the superfine sugar in a small dish. Using a small paintbrush, paint some egg white onto each flower (see figure 1) and then dip the flower into the superfine sugar (see figure 2). Place on a wire cooling rack and leave overnight to harden.

For the cupcakes
The following day, preheat the oven to 350°F.

Cream the butter and sugar together in a bowl until pale and creamy, then beat in the egg gradually. Add the rose water and sift in the flour with the baking powder, folding them into the mixture. Stir in the milk to loosen the batter a little.

Pipe or spoon the batter into the mini cake cases, about three-quarters full, bake for 8–10 minutes and then allow to cool. You can tell that the cakes are done when you lightly touch them and they bounce back (see figure 3).

For the icing
Mix the cream cheese and confectioners' sugar together and then stir in some food coloring, adding a small amount at a time until you achieve a color you like. Spoon the icing into a piping bag and then pipe onto each cake. Gently press candied flowers and petals on top (see figure 4).

Hot cross bun cupcakes

Makes 12 cupcakes   Difficulty rating 🖋

Prep time: 10 minutes
Baking time: 18–20 minutes
Decorating time: 10 minutes

For the cupcakes
3 large eggs
1/3 cup buttermilk
6 1/2 oz/13 tablespoons butter
Zest of 1 orange
6 1/2 oz/1 1/4 cups self-rising flour
1/2 teaspoon baking powder
2/3 cup almond meal
1 cup light brown sugar, lightly
  packed
2 teaspoons mixed spice
2/3 cup sultanas, golden raisins,
  or currants
1 tablespoon apricot jam
  or marmalade

For the icing
2 1/4 oz/1/4 cup cream cheese
3 tablespoons butter
1/2 cup confectioners' sugar
Zest of 1/2 orange

Equipment
Cupcake tin
12 cupcake cases
Piping bag
Plain nozzle

For the cupcakes
Preheat the oven to 350°F.

Beat the eggs in a bowl and then add the buttermilk. Melt the butter, add it to the bowl and mix well. Stir in the orange zest.

In another bowl, sift together the flour, baking powder, almond meal, sugar and mixed spice, then fold these into the wet mixture. Stir in the sultanas or raisins.

Spoon the cake batter into the cake cases, about three-quarters full, and bake for 18–20 minutes until a skewer comes out clean.

Heat the apricot jam or marmalade in a saucepan with a dash of water until it becomes liquid. Using a pastry brush, glaze the cakes while they are still warm and then allow to cool.

For the icing
Mix all the icing ingredients together. Spoon the mixture into a piping bag with a small plain nozzle and pipe a cross onto the top of each cake.

ETON MESS CUPCAKES

I love Eton mess and I love cupcakes, so I decided to mix the two together. I used both strawberries and raspberries but they can be made with either fruit. I also made mini candy-striped meringues for extra cuteness. When making meringues I prefer to weigh the ingredients for accuracy, so adjust the quantities specified as necessary — simply weigh the egg white and use double the quantity of sugar.

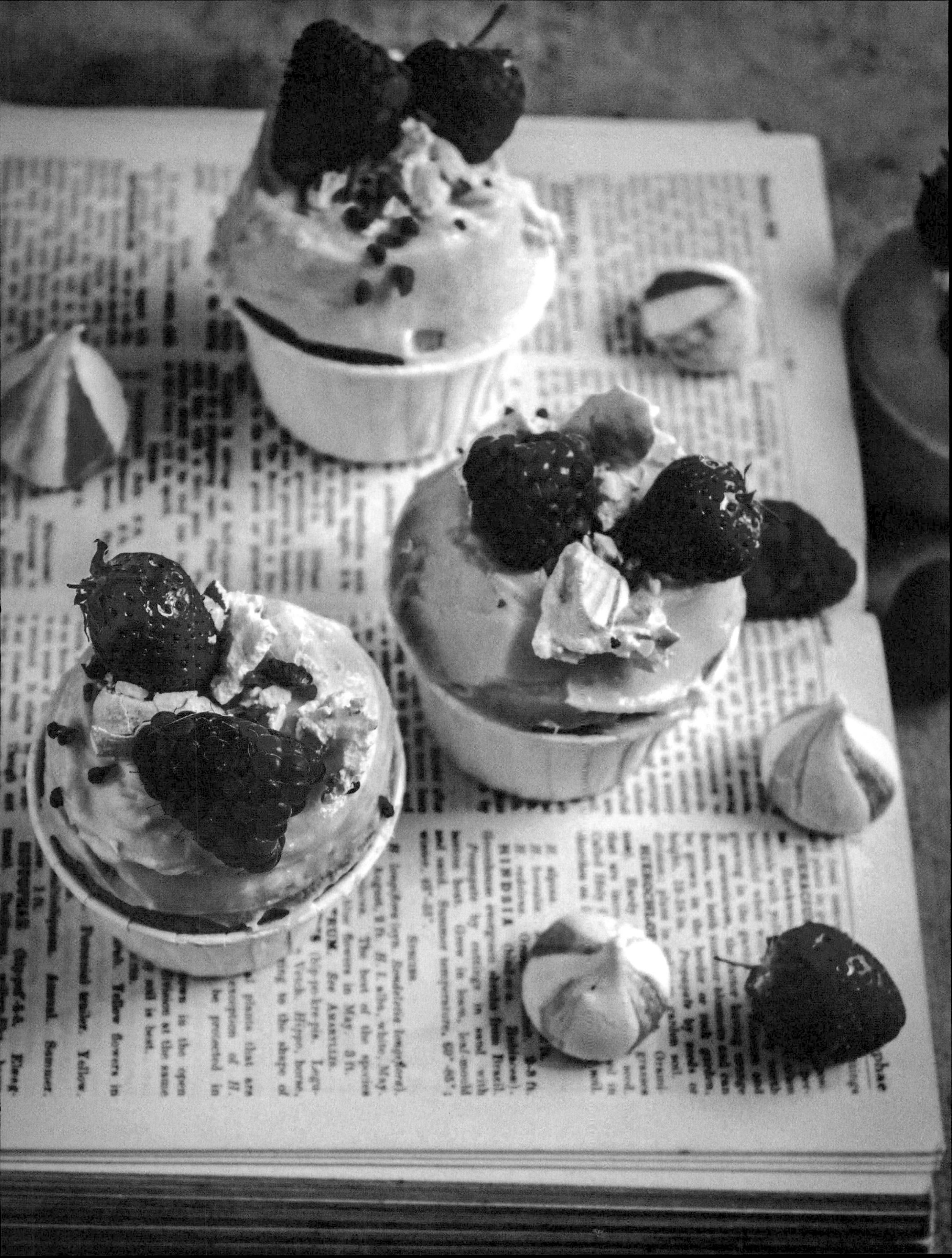

Eton mess cupcakes

Makes 6 cupcakes   Difficulty rating 🖊🖊

For the meringue kisses
$1/2$ cup superfine sugar
White of 1 egg
Pink food coloring

For the cupcakes
$4^1/2$ oz/9 tablespoons butter
$1/2$ cup superfine sugar
2 eggs
1 teaspoon vanilla extract
$3^3/4$ oz/$3/4$ cup self-rising flour
3 teaspoons milk

For the topping
$1/4$ cup heavy whipping cream
6 oz/$3/4$ cup cream cheese
Pink food coloring
$1^1/2$ cups confectioners' sugar
Fresh raspberries and
   strawberries

Equipment
Piping bag (for meringue kisses)
Baking tray (for meringue kisses)
Cupcake tin
6 cupcake cases

Prep time: 25 minutes
Baking time: meringues 40 minutes; cakes 20 minutes
Decorating time: 10 minutes

___

For the meringue kisses
Make the candy-striped meringues using the method described on page 126, piping small mounds of the meringue mixture to make mini meringue kisses. Bake for the full 40 minutes so that they are hard all the way through and easy to crumble.

For the cupcakes
Preheat the oven to 350°F.

Cream the butter and sugar together in a bowl until pale and creamy. Beat in the eggs one at a time. Add the vanilla extract, sift in the flour and fold into the mixture. Stir in the milk to loosen the batter a little.

Spoon into the cake cases until the cases are approximately three-quarters full (see figure 1), bake for 20 minutes and then allow to cool.

For the topping
Whip the cream until thick, then add the cream cheese and a small amount of pink food coloring. Sift in the confectioners' sugar and mix together. Spoon the icing onto each cupcake and smooth out to cover the top (see figure 2). Break up the meringues and sprinkle on top with fresh raspberries and strawberries (see figures 3 and 4).

1. Fill the cake cases until they are approximately three-quarters full

2. Smooth the icing over the cupcake to cover the top

3. Sprinkle crushed meringues on the cupcake

4. Top each cupcake with fresh strawberries and raspberries

Glazed blueberry muffins

Makes 6 muffins   Difficulty rating 🥄

For the muffins
$^1/_2$ cup fresh blueberries
$4^1/_2$ oz/9 tablespoons butter
$^1/_2$ cup superfine sugar
1 teaspoon vanilla extract
2 eggs
$3^3/_4$ oz/$^3/_4$ cup self-rising flour
3 teaspoons milk

For the topping
$^1/_4$ cup confectioners' sugar
Selection of edible flowers
    (I used cornflowers, but note
    that only the petals are edible)

Equipment
Fluted silicone cupcake mold
    or cases

Prep time: 10 minutes
Baking time: 15–20 minutes
Decorating time: 5 minutes

For the muffins
Preheat the oven to 350°F.

Place the blueberries on a tray and roast for about 5–8 minutes until they start to release their juice. Reserve the juice, then allow the blueberries to cool in a bowl, stirring to release more juice for the glaze.

Cream the butter and sugar together in a bowl until pale and creamy. Add the vanilla extract and beat in the eggs one at a time. Sift in the flour and fold in with the roasted blueberries (draining off and reserving any extra juice for the glaze). Stir in the milk to loosen the batter a little.

Spoon the mixture into cake cases, about three-quarters full, and bake for 15–20 minutes or until a skewer comes out clean. Allow to cool.

For the topping
Mix the reserved blueberry juice with the confectioners' sugar and use it to glaze each muffin. Decorate with a selection of fresh flowers (carefully wash and dry them first).

2. Teatime treats

Cheesecake eggs and shortbread soldiers

Makes 12 eggs and 12 soldiers   Difficulty rating 🥄

For the eggshells
12 saved eggshells

For the cheesecake
1 cup extra thick heavy cream
6 oz/³/₄ cup cream cheese
¹/₄ cup confectioners' sugar
Zest of ¹/₂ lemon
3 tablespoons lemon curd
   or marmalade

For the shortbread
6 oz/1 cup all-purpose flour
¹/₂ cup cornstarch
¹/₃ cup superfine sugar
¹/₄ teaspoon salt
4¹/₂ oz/9 tablespoons butter

Equipment
Stand mixer
8 x 8 in baking tin
Food processor

Prep time: shortbread 10 minutes; cheesecake 10 minutes
Baking time: 30 minutes
Decorating time: 5 minutes

For the eggshells
Save your eggshells from any cakes or breakfasts you make. I pull out the filmy part inside and wash them in boiling water to kill any germs. Allow to air-dry.

For the cheesecake
Put the cream and cream cheese into the bowl of a stand mixer and fold in the confectioners' sugar (I do this first or it will go everywhere when you turn on the mixer). Whip until thick and fluffy (1–2 minutes on a medium–high speed). Stir in the lemon zest.

Spoon the mixture into a piping bag and pipe some into each eggshell. Add a teaspoonful of lemon curd or marmalade for the "egg yolk."

For the shortbread
Preheat the oven to 350°F and line the baking tin with baking paper.

Put the flour, cornstarch, sugar and salt into a food processor and whizz to combine. Mix in the butter until it just starts to come together. Press the mixture into the baking tin. Slice into rectangles, prick each biscuit with a skewer and bake for 30 minutes. Remove from the oven, re-cut the rectangles and then allow to cool.

Dip the shortbread soldiers in the eggs and enjoy.

ORANGE, ROSE WATER AND SAFFRON SCONES

I think of these as the sultan's scones, as they have the flavors of the Middle East, like rose water as well as saffron, which is worth its weight in gold.

Orange, rose water and saffron scones

Makes 8 scones   Difficulty rating 🥄

For the scones
10 strands saffron
7 oz/1¹/₃ cups all-purpose flour,
   plus extra for sprinkling
¹/₂ cup granulated sugar
¹/₄ teaspoon salt
2 teaspoons baking powder
2¹/₄ oz/4¹/₂ tablespoons butter
1 large egg
¹/₄ cup Greek yogurt
¹/₄ cup orange juice
¹/₂ teaspoon orange extract
1 teaspoon orange zest
3 teaspoons rose water
2 tablespoons dried rose petals

For the glaze
1 cup confectioners' sugar
2 tablespoons orange juice
1 teaspoon orange zest

Equipment
Baking tray
Large knife or pizza cutter

Prep time: 10 minutes
Baking time: 35–40 minutes
Decorating time: 5 minutes

For the scones
Preheat the oven to 350°F and line a baking tray with baking paper.

Soak the saffron strands in 1 tablespoon of boiling water. Using an electric mixer, combine the flour, sugar, salt, baking powder and butter until the mixture resembles coarse crumbs (see figure 1). Mix in the egg, yogurt, orange juice, extract and zest (see figure 2), then add the water from the saffron and the rose water and petals and mix thoroughly (see figure 3).

Shape the dough into a large ball and place on the baking tray. Pat the dough into a flat circle and sprinkle with flour to make it workable. Using a large knife or pizza cutter, slice the dough into triangles and then bake for 25 minutes. Remove from the oven and re-cut the triangles carefully. Separate and return to the oven for another 10–15 minutes. Allow to cool completely before glazing.

For the glaze
Beat all of the glaze ingredients together in a bowl. Spoon or brush the glaze over each scone (see figure 4) and allow to set (about 15 minutes). Store in an airtight container.

1. Mix the scone ingredients until the mixture resembles coarse crumbs

2. Add the egg, yogurt, orange juice, extract and zest to the mixture

3. Incorporate the saffron, rose water and rose petals into the scone mixture

4. Drizzle the glaze over each scone and allow to set

Strawberry milkshake French toast

Makes 6 slices   Difficulty rating ✒

Prep time: 5 minutes
Cooking time: 6 minutes per slice; 15 minutes for syrup

For the toast
1 cup strawberry milk
3 eggs
1 teaspoon vanilla extract
2^1/$_4$ oz/4^1/$_2$ tablespoons butter,
   plus extra for frying
20 strawberries
6 slices of day-old brioche bread

For the syrup
^{1}/$_4$ cup superfine sugar

Equipment
Frying pan

For the toast
Mix the strawberry milk, eggs and vanilla extract together in a large dish. Melt the butter and whisk it into the mixture.

Slice some of the strawberries. Cut a pocket in each piece of bread and insert some strawberry slices. Dip the bread into the milkshake and leave for a minute so that the bread soaks it up, then flip over and repeat on the other side.

Heat a frying pan and add some butter. Place a slice of the soaked bread into the pan and fry on each side for 3 minutes until cooked and nicely browned.

For the syrup
Chop the remaining strawberries and add to a saucepan with the sugar and 1 tablespoon of water. Boil over a low heat for about 10 minutes until you get a thick syrup. Press the syrup through a sieve, then pour it over the French toast and enjoy.

NANAIMO BARS

Nanaimo bars are a Canadian treat consisting of a biscuit layer, a buttercream layer and a chocolate layer. I am lucky enough to have a family member who lived in Canada so I grew up eating them. My brothers and I adore them, and I know my partner does too because he begs me to make them all the time, which I don't mind doing as they are so easy. Normally the base layer has an egg in it, but I prefer it without.

Nanaimo bars

Makes 16 bars   Difficulty rating 🍴

For the base layer
3 tablespoons chopped walnuts
2 cups graham cracker or vanilla
   wafer cookie crumbs
3 tablespoons unsweetened
   cocoa powder
$1/4$ cup superfine sugar
1 teaspoon vanilla extract
$1/2$ cup shredded coconut
$61/2$ oz/13 tablespoons butter

For the middle layer
9 oz/18 tablespoons butter
2–3 teaspoons milk or cream
$11/2$ tablespoons custard powder
$1/2$ teaspoon vanilla extract
$22/3$ cups confectioners' sugar

For the top layer
$31/2$ oz dark chocolate, chopped
1 tablespoon butter

Equipment
Food processor
8 x 8 in baking tin

Prep time: Base layer 10 minutes; middle and top layers
5 minutes each
Baking time: 10 minutes
Assembly time: 10 minutes, plus 1 hour chilling

_____

For the base layer
Preheat the oven to 350°F and line the baking tin with baking
paper.

Chop the walnuts and crush the biscuits in a food processor
and pulse until you get a fine crumb mixture. Add the cocoa,
sugar, vanilla extract and coconut (see figure 1) and pulse to
combine. Melt the butter, add it to the dry ingredients and
mix thoroughly.

Press the mixture into the baking tin (see figure 2) and bake for
10 minutes. The mixture will rise a little, so press it back down as
soon as you remove the tray from the oven. Allow it to cool and
form a solid base.

For the middle layer
Whisk the ingredients for the middle layer together until
smooth, then spread over the cooled base layer (see figure 3).
Refrigerate for 30 minutes before making the top layer.

For the top layer
Melt the chocolate and butter in a microwave or in a heat-proof
bowl over a pan of boiling water. Pour the melted chocolate over
the middle layer (see figure 4) and refrigerate for 30 minutes,
then slice and enjoy.

1. Add cocoa powder, sugar, vanilla extract and coconut and pulse to combine

2. Press the mixture into the baking tin

3. Smooth the cream mixture over the base

4. Smooth the chocolate layer over the cream

SAMOA BROWNIES

Samoas are American Girl Scout cookies consisting of a cookie covered in caramel and toasted coconut. To create these amazing treats, I added a caramel and toasted coconut topping to a batch of brownies and decorated them with melted chocolate.

Samoa brownies

Makes 9 brownies   Difficulty rating 🥄

For the brownies
3¹/₄ oz/6 tablespoons butter

7 oz/1¹/₃ cups chopped dark
   chocolate, chopped

4 eggs

1 cup superfine sugar

3³/₄ oz/³/₄ cup all-purpose flour

3 tablespoons unsweetened
   cocoa powder

1 teaspoon baking powder

For the caramel
1 cup shredded coconut

2¹/₄ oz/4¹/₂ tablespoons butter

¹/₂ cup superfine sugar

¹/₂ cup brown sugar, lightly
   packed

¹/₂ cup corn syrup

¹/₂ cup sweetened condensed
   milk

To decorate
3¹/₂ oz chocolate, chopped

Equipment
Food processor

8 x 8 in baking tin

Prep time: 20 minutes

Cooking time: Brownies 25–30 minutes; topping 10 minutes

Decorating time: 10 minutes

For the brownies
Preheat the oven to 350°F and line the baking tin with baking paper.

Melt the butter and chocolate in a microwave or in a heat-proof bowl over a pan of boiling water, then set aside to cool. Beat the eggs and sugar together in a bowl until pale and thick, then fold in the chocolate mixture. Sift in the flour, cocoa and baking powder and fold in until you have a consistent batter, but do not overmix.

Pour the mixture into the prepared baking tin. Bake for 25–30 minutes and then allow to cool.

For the caramel
Spread the desiccated coconut on a baking tray and bake for 5 minutes until toasted. Put the remaining ingredients for the caramel into a heatproof bowl and microwave for 6 minutes, stirring after every 2 minutes.

Spread half of the caramel over the brownies (see figure 1). Mix the remaining caramel with half of the toasted coconut (see figure 2) and spread this on top of the plain caramel (see figure 3). Sprinkle the remaining toasted coconut on top.

To decorate
Melt the chocolate and pipe lines over the top (see figure 4). Slice and enjoy.

1. Spread half the caramel over the baked and cooled brownies

2. Mix the remaining caramel with the shredded coconut

3. Spread the caramel and coconut mixture over the brownies

4. Pipe diagonal lines of melted chocolate over the brownies

Cherry almond chocolate blondies

Makes 8 blondies   Difficulty rating 🖋

For the blondies
3¹/₂ oz/²/₃ cup pitted and halved
  fresh cherries, plus extra for
  the top
2 eggs
¹/₂ cup brown sugar, lightly
  packed
1 teaspoon vanilla extract
1 teaspoon almond extract
3¹/₄ oz/6 tablespoons butter
3¹/₂ oz/³/₄ cup all-purpose flour
²/₃ cup chocolate chips
4 tablespoons flaked almonds,
  plus extra for sprinkling
Pinch of salt

For the icing
¹/₂ cup confectioners' sugar

Equipment
8 in round baking tin

Prep time: 10 minutes
Baking time: 25 minutes
Decorating time: 5 minutes

For the blondies
Preheat the oven to 350°F.

Grease the baking tin or line it with baking paper. Spread out the cherry halves in the base of the tin.

Beat the eggs and sugar together in a bowl until thick, then stir in the vanilla and almond extracts. Melt the butter. Adding a quarter of the butter at a time, fold it into the mixture. Add the flour, chocolate chips, almonds and salt and mix to combine.

Pour the mixture into the baking tin, add a few more cherries on top and sprinkle on some more almonds. Bake for 25 minutes and then allow to cool.

For the icing
Mix the confectioners' sugar with a few drops of water and drizzle it over the top. Slice into wedges.

BAKED BANANA CHOCOLATE CHIP DOUGHNUTS

❧❦❧

I love banana bread and am always looking for new ways to eat it, so when I had some ripe bananas that needed using up, I made these banana bread doughnuts with chocolate chips and smothered them in caramel and pecans.

Baked banana chocolate chip doughnuts

Makes 8 doughnuts   *Difficulty rating* 🥄

For the doughnuts
2¼ oz/4½ tablespoons butter
½ cup brown sugar, lightly
    packed
2 medium bananas
½ cup Greek yogurt or
    buttermilk
2 eggs
9 oz/1⅔ cups all-purpose flour
1 teaspoon baking powder
⅓ cup chocolate chips

For the topping
1 (14 oz) can dulce de leche
    (such as Carnation Caramel);
    see page 120 if you want to
    make your own
Handful of chopped pecans

Equipment
Piping bag
Doughnut tin
Cooling rack

Prep time: 10 minutes
Baking time: 13 minutes
Decorating time: 10 minutes

For the doughnuts
Preheat the oven to 350°F and grease the circles of the doughnut tin.

Cream the butter and sugar together in a bowl until pale and creamy. Mash the bananas. Add the bananas and yogurt to the bowl and mix well. Beat in the eggs. Sift in the flour and baking powder and fold in. Stir in the chocolate chips (see figure 1).

Spoon the mixture into a piping bag (see figure 2) and pipe circles of dough into the doughnut tin (see figure 3). Bake for 13 minutes and then allow to cool on a cooling rack.

For the topping
Use a spoon to spread dulce de leche onto each doughnut (see figure 4) and then sprinkle with chopped pecans.

1. Stir the chocolate chips into the mixture

2. Spoon doughnut mixture into a piping bag

3. Pipe circles of dough into a doughnut tin

4. Spoon dulce de leche over each doughnut

LONDON FOG MILLEFEUILLES

❧ ⬧ ☙

This recipe was inspired by a London fog latte, which is an Earl Grey and vanilla bean latte. I added lavender as I think it goes well with the flavor of Earl Grey, which I love. Being from England, I grew up drinking it, so I like finding new ways to enjoy it.

The pastry cream filling is infused with Earl Grey tea and vanilla, and the whipped cream is flavored with lavender extract. I made my own puff pastry but store-bought pastry is fine. The top layer is decorated with feathered icing, but you can just dust with confectioners' sugar if you prefer.

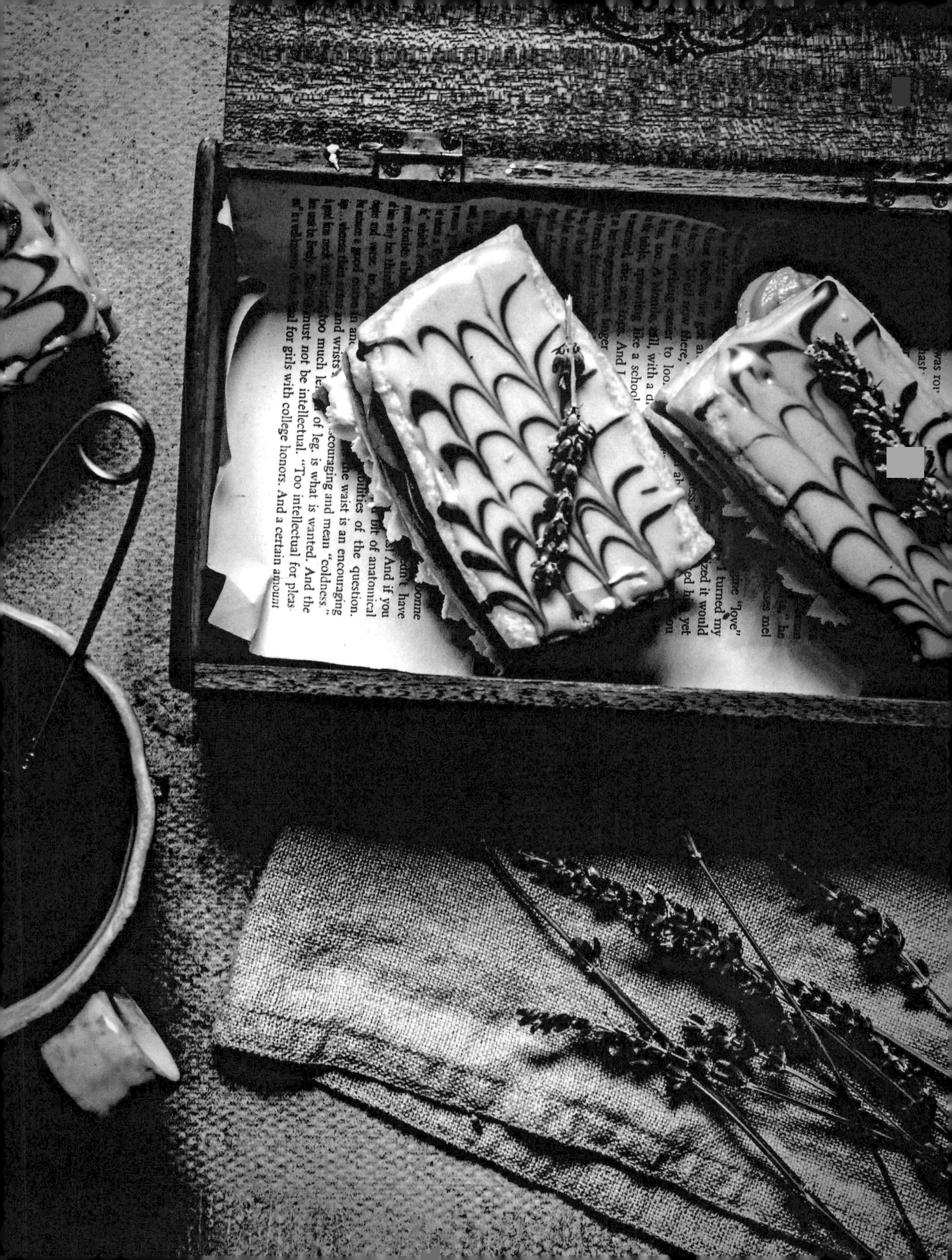

London fog millefeuilles

Makes 6 millefeuilles   Difficulty rating *f f f*

For the puff pastry
9 oz/1²/₃ cups all-purpose flour
1 teaspoon salt
Juice of ¹/₄ lemon
¹/₃ cup cold water
7 oz block of butter (you need
    the butter in one piece)

For the pastry cream
1 cup milk
2 Earl Grey tea bags
2 vanilla pods
3 egg yolks
¹/₄ cup superfine sugar
1¹/₂ tablespoons cornstarch

For the lavender cream
³/₄ cup whipping cream
3 tablespoons confectioners'
    sugar
¹/₂ teaspoon lavender extract

To decorate
1 cup confectioners' sugar
Lilac food coloring
6 sprigs lavender (carefully
    washed and dried)

Prep time: 30 minutes, plus 2 hours resting
Baking time: 30 minutes
Decorating time: 30 minutes

For the puff pastry
Put the flour and salt into a bowl, add the lemon juice and water and knead until smooth. Shape into a ball and make two cuts in the form of a cross to half the depth of the dough (see figure 1). Put the dough into a plastic bag and refrigerate for 1 hour.

Place the block of butter between two sheets of baking paper and use a rolling pin to flatten it into a thin square. Remove the dough from the fridge, pull each cut section outwards and roll out into a large diamond shape. Place the butter in the center, fold the corners of the dough over it like an envelope and press the edges together (see figure 2). Roll out the dough into a large rectangle (see figure 3), fold each end to the center (see figure 4) and then fold in half (this is called a book fold).

Rotate the dough 90 degrees and roll out into a rectangle again. Fold over a third of the dough to the center (see figure 5), then fold the rest over the top (see figure 6). Wrap in plastic wrap and refrigerate for 30 minutes. Repeat this process four more times. After the final refrigeration, fold the dough into thirds once more and then the puff pastry is ready to use.

1. Make two cross cuts to half the depth of the dough

2. Fold the corners of the dough over the butter to the center. This is called an envelope fold

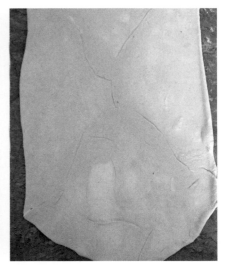

3. Roll the dough out into a large rectangle

4. Fold each end of the rectangle to the center

5. Fold a third of the dough to the center

6. Fold the other third over top. Wrap in plastic wrap and refrigerate

Equipment

Rolling pin
2 baking trays
Cooling rack
2 piping bags
Bamboo or metal skewer

Preheat the oven to 400°F and line a baking tray with baking paper. Roll out the pastry to fit the tray and slice into 18 rectangles. Place another baking tray on top to weigh down the pastry. Bake for 20 minutes, then turn the baking tray and bake for another 10 minutes. Set aside and allow to cool.

For the pastry cream and lavender cream

Make the pastry cream filling using the method described on page 83, adding the tea bags to the milk along with the vanilla pod and also removing them at the same time. Whip the ingredients for the lavender cream together to form stiff peaks. Spoon each cream filling into a piping bag.

To build the millefeuilles, pipe lavender cream onto six of the pastry rectangles. Add another layer of pastry on top and pipe the pastry cream onto this (see figure 7). Add a top layer of pastry.

To decorate

Mix the confectioners sugar with 3–4 teaspoons of water to make a thick icing. Stir in a small amount of food coloring to create a pale lilac color. Separate a little of the icing into another bowl and add a little more food coloring to make a darker lilac. Spread pale lilac icing over the top of each millefeuille (see figure 8). Put the darker lilac icing into a piping bag and pipe lines across each pastry (see figure 9). Lightly drag a bamboo or metal skewer across the piped lines to feather them (see figure 10). Add a sprig of lavender on top.

7. For each millefeuille, pipe one layer of lavender cream and one layer of pastry cream

8. Spread pale lilac icing over the top of the millefeuille

9. To make a feathered pattern, pipe lines of the darker icing across each pastry

10. Lightly drag a skewer across the piped lines to feather them

OREO MACARONS

If you like Oreos and macarons like I do then I really recommend that you give these a go. I enjoy making macarons at home and prefer homemade ones to the shop-bought variety. I always weigh my ingredients for macarons because the measurements need to be precise.

Oreo macarons

Makes 25 macarons   Difficulty rating 🥄🥄

For the macaron shells
1 cup almond meal
1²/₃ cups confectioners' sugar
3 tablespoons Oreo crumbs
(pull the Oreos apart and use
the halves without the cream
filling; you will need 3–4
halves)
¹/₄ cup egg whites
¹/₂ teaspoon salt
¹/₄ cup superfine sugar
Black food coloring

For the buttercream
10 Oreo cookies
6¹/₂ oz/13 tablespoons butter
¹/₄ cup confectioners' sugar

Equipment
Baking tray
Food processor
2 piping bags

Prep time: 10 minutes
Resting time: 20–60 minutes
Baking and assembly: 30 minutes

For the macaron shells
Preheat the oven to 275°F and line the baking tray with baking paper or use a macaron mat.

Put the almond meal into the food processor and pulse, then add the confectioners' sugar and pulse again to form a fine powder (see figure 1). Transfer to a bowl for later. Put the Oreo halves into the food processor and pulse to a fine crumb. Stir into the almond mixture.

Whip the egg whites and salt until foamy, then add the superfine sugar a spoonful at a time. Whip until the mixture forms stiff peaks. Add a small amount of black food coloring to make the mixture a grey color (see figure 2). Sift in a quarter of the almond mixture and fold in (see figure 3), then repeat until it is all combined (try not to overwork the mixture).

Spoon into a piping bag and pipe circles onto the baking tray. Tap the baking tray on the worktop a few times to pop any air bubbles, then leave the macarons for 20–60 minutes to form a skin. Bake the macarons for 20 minutes and then allow to cool.

For the buttercream
Put 10 whole Oreos into the food processor and pulse to a fine crumb. Beat the butter in a bowl until soft, then mix in the confectioners' sugar and Oreo crumbs (but reserve some of the crumbs for sprinkling). Spoon the buttercream into a piping bag. Pipe buttercream onto half the macaron shells (see figure 4), sprinkle with Oreo crumbs and sandwich another macaron shell on top.

1. Pulse the almonds and confectioners' sugar to form a fine powder

2. Whip the egg whites, salt, sugar and a touch of black food coloring until the mixture forms stiff peaks

3. Sift in the almond mixture a quarter at a time, but try not to overwork the mixture

4. Pipe the buttercream onto half of the macaron shells

ENGLISH MADELEINES

I remember having these at school when I was a little girl. They are quite an old-fashioned cake that you don't see very often any more, which is a shame because they are wonderful. They are a bit like Australian lamingtons, but they are brushed with jam rather than chocolate. I used dariole molds to bake them in, but you can use a silicone cupcake mold if you prefer.

English madeleines

For the cakes
3¹/₄ oz/6¹/₂ tablespoons butter
¹/₂ cup superfine sugar
2 eggs
1 teaspoon vanilla extract
3¹/₂ oz/²/₃ cup self-rising flour
1 teaspoon baking powder

For the coating
4 tablespoons raspberry jam
1 cup shredded coconut

Equipment
6 dariole molds or silicone
   cupcake mold
Fork

Prep time: 10 minutes
Baking time: 20–25 minutes
Decorating time: 15 minutes

For the cakes
Preheat the oven to 350°F.

Cream the butter and sugar together in a bowl until pale and creamy. Beat in the eggs one at a time, then stir in the vanilla extract. Sift in the flour and baking powder and fold into the mixture.

Grease each dariole mold and line the bottom with baking paper. Fill each mold a little over half full with the cake mixture (see figure 1). Bake for 20–25 minutes until firm and golden (see figure 2), then remove from the molds and allow to cool.

Slice the risen tops off the cakes and turn upside down.

For the coating
Press the jam through a sieve into a saucepan. Warm the jam and brush some onto each cake (see figure 3). Roll the cakes in coconut, using a fork to hold them (see figure 4).

1. Fill each mold so it is a little over half full

2. Remove the golden cakes from the molds and trim the risen tops

3. Brush some warm jam onto each cake

4. Roll the cakes in coconut

Red velvet madeleines

Makes 10 madeleines   Difficulty rating 🥄

2¹/₄ oz/4¹/₂ tablespoons butter,
   plus extra
   for greasing molds
Red food coloring
4 tablespoons superfine sugar
1³/₄ oz/¹/₃ cup all-purpose flour,
   plus extra for dusting molds
¹/₂ teaspoon baking powder
Pinch of salt
2 teaspoons unsweetened
   cocoa powder
1 egg
2 teaspoons buttermilk
Confectioners' sugar, for dusting

Equipment
Madeleine molds

Prep time: 10 minutes, plus 1 hour chilling
Baking time: 8–10 minutes
Decorating time: 2 minutes

Put the butter into a saucepan to melt and stir in a small amount of red food coloring. Mix the sugar, 1 oz/¹/₄ cup flour, baking powder, salt and cocoa together in a bowl. Pour in the melted butter, add the egg and stir. Mix in the buttermilk and the remaining flour. Cover with plastic wrap and refrigerate for at least 1 hour.

Brush the madeleine molds with more melted butter and sift over some flour. Tap the molds to remove excess flour and place them in the fridge for 1 hour.

Preheat the oven to 350°F.

Spoon the cake batter into the molds so that each is three-quarters full. Bake for 8–10 minutes and then allow to cool. Dust with confectioners' sugar.

CROQUEMBOUCHE

❧⟐❧

The word croquembouche means crack or crunch in the mouth. There's something about croquembouche that always looks so appealing. I had been wanting to make one for a while, so one weekend I finally got around to it. The result was beautiful. I can see why in France they have it as their traditional wedding cake. I used flowers to decorate mine, but traditionally it would be decorated with spun sugar. It is not as hard to make as you might think, but there are several stages to it.

Croquembouche

Serves 8–10   Difficulty rating 🍥🍥🍥

Prep time: 20 minutes
Baking time: 30–45 minutes
Construction time: 50 minutes

For the candied flowers
Selection of edible flowers, such
   as primroses and violets
$1/4$ cup superfine sugar
2 oz egg white (about
   1 egg white)

For the choux pastry
$6^1/2$ oz/$1^1/4$ cups all-purpose flour
$1^1/2$ tablespoons superfine sugar
$1/4$ teaspoon salt
$4^1/2$ oz/9 tablespoons butter
1 cup water
4 eggs

For the pastry cream
1 cup milk
1 vanilla pod
3 egg yolks
$1/4$ cup superfine sugar
3 teaspoons cornstarch
3 teaspoons custard powder (if
   you don't have any, add more
   cornstarch instead)

For the caramel
1 cup superfine sugar
1 tablespoon water

For the candied flowers
Wash the flowers and dry them gently. Place the superfine sugar in a small dish. Using a small paintbrush, paint some egg white onto each flower and then dip the flower into the superfine sugar. Place on a wire cooling rack and leave overnight to harden.

For the choux pastry
Preheat the oven to 375°F and line the two baking trays with baking paper.

Combine the flour, sugar and salt in a bowl. Heat the butter and water in a saucepan, stirring until the butter has melted. Remove from the heat and quickly add the dry ingredients, stirring constantly. Using a wooden spoon, beat the mixture until it forms a ball of paste that pulls away from the sides of the pan, then return the pan to the heat and stir for another minute or two.

Transfer the mixture to the bowl of the stand mixer and allow to cool for 5 minutes. Beat the eggs in another bowl. Turn on the mixer and slowly add the eggs. At first it will look like the eggs will not mix in, but stick with it until you achieve a smooth, glossy paste.

Spoon the paste into a piping bag with a plain nozzle (see figure 1) and pipe small mounds onto the baking trays, leaving gaps between them (see figure 2). Smooth down the top of each mound with a finger dipped in water (see figure 3).

1. Spoon choux pastry into a piping bag

2. Pipe small mounds onto the baking tray

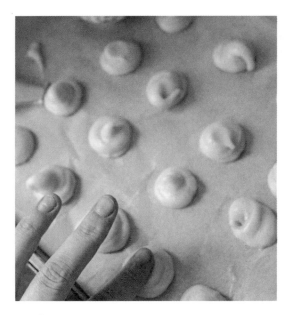

3. Smooth down the top of each mound with a finger dipped in water

4. Use a knife or skewer to prick a hole in each choux bun and return them to the oven

5. Pipe the pastry cream into the choux buns

6. Brush down the sides of the pan to stop the sugar from burning

7. Dip the filled choux buns in the hot caramel

8. Construct the croquembouche by arranging the buns in a circle, building the croquembouche up into a cone

Equipment

Small paintbrush
Cooling rack
2 baking trays
Stand mixer
2 piping bags
Pastry brush
Candy thermometer (optional)
2 forks

Turn the oven down to 350°F and bake for 25–35 minutes until golden brown. Remove from the oven and use a knife or skewer to prick a hole in each choux bun (see figure 4). Lower the temperature to 325°F and return the buns to the oven for another 5–10 minutes to dry out.

For the pastry cream

Set a bowl over ice water. Pour the milk into a saucepan over a low heat. Score the vanilla pod, remove the seeds and add both to the milk. Mix the egg yolks, sugar, cornstarch and custard powder (if using) together in another bowl.

Turn up the heat and bring the milk to a boil. Remove the vanilla pod and then whisk the hot milk into the egg mixture. Pour the mixture back into the pan over a low heat, stirring constantly until it thickens. Press the mixture through a sieve into the bowl over ice water. Cover with plastic wrap, touching the surface of the custard so that a skin does not form, and allow to cool completely. Spoon the cool pastry cream into a piping bag and pipe some into each choux bun (see figure 5).

For the caramel

Fill the sink with cold water ready for the pan. Heat the sugar and water in a heavy-based saucepan over a low heat, stirring until the sugar has dissolved. Use a pastry brush dipped in cold water to wash any sugar crystals from the sides of the pan down into the syrup (see figure 6). Continue until the mixture turns golden amber. You can check that it is ready by dropping some into a cup of cold water to see if it forms a hard ball. Alternatively, use a sugar thermometer and heat the sugar to 255°F.

Once the caramel is ready, put the pan into the sink of cold water. Take a choux bun, dip it in the caramel (see figure 7) and start building the croquembouche. Begin with a circle of buns and build them up into a cone shape (see figure 8).

Using two forks that have been dipped in the caramel, spin the sugar and wrap the strands of sugar around the croquembouche. Reheat the caramel if you need to.

Decorate with the candied flowers.

BLUEBERRY AND LAVENDER RELIGIEUSE

I was inspired to make these religieuse after a trip to a Parisian-style café in London's Covent Garden, an outpost of the Parisian patisserie Ladurée, famous for its macarons. I filled the buns with a mixture of whipped cream and blueberry syrup rather than the pastry cream traditionally used with choux pastry.

Blueberry and lavender religieuse

Makes 6 pastries   Difficulty rating 𝓟 𝓟

For the choux pastry
6¹/2 oz/1¹/4 cups all-purpose flour
1¹/2 tablespoons superfine sugar
¹/4 teaspoon salt
4¹/2 oz/9 tablespoons butter
1 cup water
4 eggs

For the cream filling
2 cups whipping cream
¹/4 cup confectioners' sugar
1 cup blueberries, plus extra for
   decorating
¹/4 cup superfine sugar
¹/2 teaspoon lavender extract

To decorate
6 oz purple rolled fondant
¹/2 cup confectioners' sugar
6 sprigs of lavender (washed
   and carefully dried)

Equipment
2 piping bags
Rolling pin

Prep time: 20 minutes
Baking time: 35–45 minutes
Decorating time: 25 minutes

For the choux pastry
Make six small and six larger choux pastry buns (see figure 1) using the method described on pages 80–83.

For the cream filling
To make the cream filling, whip the cream and confectioners' sugar together until stiff. Heat the blueberries, sugar and lavender extract until the blueberries break down. Purée in a blender, press through a sieve and then stir into the cream. Pipe some filling into each bun, reserving a small amount for assembling the pastries.

To decorate
Roll out the fondant and cut out circles to go on top of each bun (see figure 2). Pipe a dot of cream filling onto each larger bun and then place a small bun on top (see figure 3).

Mix the confectioner' sugar with 2 teaspoons of water and pipe lines of white icing across the smaller buns. Top each pastry with a blueberry and a sprig of lavender (see figure 4).

1. Make both large and small choux buns

2. Cut fondant circles to go on top of each filled choux bun

3. Pipe a dot of pastry cream on top of the larger bun and place the small bun on top

4. Pipe lines of white icing across the smaller bun and decorate with a blueberry and a sprig of lavender.

VIOLET AND LEMON ÉCLAIRS

I made these pastries with a vintage éclair tin that I found online. I just love vintage baking tins — I always think they must have such a history and imagine all the kitchens they may have been in. My mum and grandma picked these violets for me while they were on a dog walk.

Violet and lemon éclairs

Makes 12 éclairs   Difficulty rating 🍴🍴

For the candied violets
24 violets
$1/4$ cup superfine sugar
1 egg white

For the choux pastry
$6^1/2$ oz/$1^1/4$ cups all-purpose flour
$1^1/2$ tablespoons superfine sugar
$1/4$ teaspoon salt
$4^1/2$ oz/9 tablespoons butter
1 cup water
4 eggs

For the pastry cream
1 cup whipping cream
Zest of $1/2$ lemon
$1^1/2$ tablespoons lemon juice
$2^1/4$ tablespoons confectioners' sugar

For the icing
1 cup confectioners' sugar
Purple food coloring

Equipment
Small paintbrush
Cooling rack
2 piping bags
Baking tray or éclair tin

Prep time: Flowers: 10 minutes, plus overnight to harden; éclairs: 20 minutes
Baking time: 35–45 minutes
Decorating time: 10 minutes

For the candied violets
Wash the flowers and dry them gently. Place the superfine sugar in a small dish. Using a small paintbrush, paint some egg white onto each flower and then dip the flower into the superfine sugar. Place on a wire cooling rack and leave overnight to harden.

For the choux pastry
Make the choux pastry éclairs using the method described on pages 80–83, piping a 5-inch line of the mixture for each éclair either in an éclair tin or on a greased baking tray (see figure 1).

For the pastry cream
To make the cream filling, whip the cream until it forms soft peaks. Add the lemon zest, juice and confectioners' sugar and continue to whip until stiff peaks form. Pipe the cream into the éclairs (see figure 2).

For the icing
To decorate the éclairs, mix the confectioners' sugar with 3–4 teaspoons of water. Stir in some food coloring, adding a small amount at a time until you achieve a color you like (see figure 3). Spread icing along the top of each éclair (see figure 4) or dip them into the icing. Place two candied violets onto the icing at one end of each éclair.

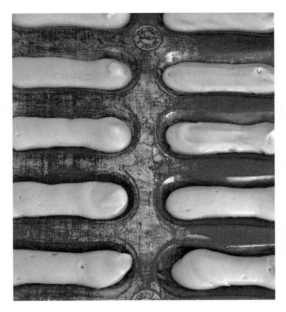

1. Pipe 13 cm (5 in) lines of mixture for each éclair on either an éclair tin or a greased baking tray

2. Pipe the pastry cream into the éclairs

3. Mix the confectioners' sugar with water. Add a small amount of food color until you achieve the color you like

4. Spread icing along the top of each éclair

3. Cookies and confectionery

Blueberry macaroon thumbprints

Makes 10–12 cookies   Difficulty rating 🥄

For the thumbprints
1/4 cup blueberries

1/3 cup superfine sugar, plus
   2 tablespoons for blueberry
   sauce

2 1/4 cups shredded coconut, or
   1 2/3 cups shredded coconut
   plus 1/2 cup sliced blanched
   almonds

Pinch of salt

3 egg whites

1 teaspoon almond extract

Shredded coconut and sliced
   blanched almonds, for
   sprinkling

For the jam
5 peaches

1 cup granulated sugar

Equipment
Baking tray

Food processor

Blender

Prep time: 10 minutes
Baking time: 25 minutes
Jam: 10 minutes

For the thumbprints
Preheat the oven to 350°F and line the baking tray with baking paper.

Put the blueberries into a saucepan with 1 tablespoon of water and 2 tablespoons of superfine sugar. Simmer until a thick sauce forms, then press through a sieve. Allow the sauce to cool.

Put the coconut and almonds into a food processor and pulse to chop the almonds. Add the remaining sugar, salt, egg whites and almond extract and pulse to combine. To create a marbled effect, remove half the mixture, stir the blueberry sauce into it and then carefully swirl this back into the rest of the mixture (this is not essential and you can mix the two together to achieve a uniform color if you prefer).

Roll balls of the mixture and push your thumb into the center to make thumbprints. Sprinkle almonds and coconut on top. Bake for 25 minutes and then allow to cool.

For the jam
Peel and chop the peaches and purée in a blender. Pour the peach purée into a saucepan with the sugar. Simmer for about 10 minutes on a low to medium heat until reduced and thick. Spoon some jam into each thumbprint.

MUSHROOM-SHAPED GINGERBREAD COOKIES

I adore lebkuchen, though I can never pronounce the name. These popular German gingerbread-type cookies are usually seen in shops around Christmas time. I thought it would be fun to make them into mushroom shapes, which would be great for a woodland-themed party. I was going to put them on top of a Black Forest gateau but they were so good that we ate them before I had the chance to make the cake.

Mushroom-shaped gingerbread cookies

Makes 12 cookies   Difficulty rating 🥄

For the cookies

1 whole egg plus 1 egg yolk

1 cup superfine sugar

7 oz/1$^{1}/_{3}$ cups all-purpose flour

1$^{1}/_{4}$ cups almond meal

1$^{1}/_{2}$ tablespoons unsweetened
   cocoa powder

3 teaspoons ground cinnamon

1$^{1}/_{2}$ teaspoons ground cardamom

1$^{1}/_{2}$ teaspoons ground ginger

$^{3}/_{4}$ teaspoon ground cloves

$^{3}/_{4}$ teaspoon ground nutmeg

4 tablespoons mixed peel

To decorate

3$^{1}/_{4}$ cups confectioners' sugar

4 oz dark chocolate, chopped

Equipment

2 baking trays

Wire rack

Paintbrush

Prep time: 10 minutes, plus 20 minutes chilling

Baking time: 15–20 minutes

Decorating time: 30 minutes

For the cookies

Line the baking trays with baking paper. Whisk the egg, yolk and superfine sugar together in a heat-proof bowl over a saucepan of gently simmering water until thick and foamy. Remove from the heat and continue to whisk for 2 minutes. Sift the flour, almonds, cocoa and spices into the mixture, then add the mixed peel and fold in. Roll the dough into a ball, cover with plastic wrap and refrigerate for 20 minutes.

Preheat the oven to 350°F. Flour your work surface and split the dough in half (see figure 1). Roll one half into small balls for the mushroom caps. Roll the other half into tapered logs for the mushroom stalks (see figure 2). Vary the sizes for a more realistic effect. Bake for 15–20 minutes, then allow to cool on a wire rack.

To decorate

Mix a few drops of water into a quarter of the confectioners' sugar to make a thick paste. Use the icing to glue the tops of the stalks to the mushroom caps and allow to dry (see figure 3).

Reserve a little confectioners' sugar for sprinkling, then mix the remaining sugar with 1 teaspoon of water at a time to make an icing that is wet enough to coat the cookies but not so thin that it will run off. Dip the mushrooms in the icing and allow to dry (see figure 4).

Sprinkle the mushrooms with a little confectioners' sugar and cocoa to look like mud. Melt the chocolate in a microwave or in a heat-proof bowl over a pan of boiling water. Use a paintbrush to brush chocolate onto the underside of the mushroom caps.

1. On a floured worktop, split your dough in half

2. Vary the sizes of the caps and stalks and bake on a paper-lined baking tray

3. Put a little icing onto the tops of the stalks and press them onto the mushroom caps. Allow to dry

4. Dip the whole mushroom in icing and allow to dry

COCONUT BROWNIE COOKIES

These coconut-filled cookies are delicious and the cookie tastes just like a brownie. To make them even more naughty I dipped them in chocolate. If you like coconut and brownies, then these are for you.

Coconut brownie cookies

Makes 9 cookies   Difficulty rating 🥄

For the cookies
6 oz dark chocolate, chopped
2¹/₂ oz/4¹/₂ tablespoons butter
2 eggs
²/₃ cup superfine sugar
3 teaspoons vanilla extract
6¹/₂ oz/1¹/₄ cups all-purpose flour
1¹/₂ teaspoons baking powder
3 tablespoons unsweetened
   cocoa powder

For the filling and topping
1 cup shredded coconut, plus
   extra for sprinkling
¹/₄ cup confectioners' sugar
1 (14 oz) can of sweetened
   condensed milk
8 oz chocolate, for dipping

Equipment
Baking tray

Prep time: 20 minutes, plus at least 2 hours chilling or overnight
Baking time: 12–15 minutes
Decorating time: 20 minutes

For the cookies
Melt the dark chocolate and butter together in a microwave or in a heatproof bowl placed over a pan of boiling water, then set aside to cool.

Whisk the eggs and superfine sugar together in a bowl until pale and creamy. Stir in the cooled chocolate and the vanilla extract, then sift in the flour and baking powder and mix well. The mixture will be like a thick cake batter. Cover with plastic wrap and refrigerate for at least 2 hours or overnight.

Preheat the oven to 315°F and line two baking trays with baking paper.

The cookie mixture should now be firm, with a chocolate truffle consistency. Take a small handful of the mixture and roll it into a ball, then roll the ball in cocoa and place on a baking tray. Roll 18 balls of dough in this way and refrigerate for 10 minutes. Bake for 12–15 minutes until the cookies are firm on the outside and soft on the inside.

For the filling and topping
Put the coconut and confectioners' sugar into a bowl, then gradually mix in the condensed milk, adding a little at a time until the mixture comes together and can be rolled into balls. Spoon the mixture onto the flat side of one cookie (see figure 1). Sandwich a ball of filling between two cookies and set aside (see figure 2). Melt the chocolate and dip the cookies halfway into it (see figure 3). Sprinkle on a line of coconut (see figure 4) and allow to harden.

1. Mix in the condensed milk until the mixture can be rolled into balls. Spoon the mixture onto the flat side of one brownie cookie

2. Sandwich the coconut filling between two brownie cookies

3. Melt chocolate, and dip each cookie halfway into the melted chocolate

4. Sprinkle a line of coconut and allow the chocolate to harden

Nutty granola balls

Makes 12 to 15 balls   Difficulty rating 🥄

¹/₃ cup peanuts

1 cup muesli (granola)

¹/₄ cup rolled oats

3 tablespoons sunflower seeds

¹/₄ cup dried cranberries and/or
 other dried fruit

¹/₃ cup peanut

3 tablespoons runny honey, plus
 extra if necessary

Equipment

Food processor

Baking tray

Prep time: 10 minutes
Baking time: 12 minutes

Preheat the oven to 350°F and line the baking tray with baking paper.

In the food processor pulse the peanuts until chopped. In a bowl combine the muesli, oats, seeds, dried fruits and chopped peanuts. Add the peanut butter and honey to the dry ingredients and mix, adding more honey if needed to make the mixture clump together.

Roll the mixture into balls and place on the baking tray. Bake for 6 minutes on each side.

SYRUP-SOAKED TURKISH SHORTBREAD

These little shortbreads are really easy to make and they taste wonderful. Soaking them in lemon and rose water syrup gives them a texture that is soft but still crunchy.

Syrup-soaked Turkish shortbread

Makes 12 biscuits *Difficulty rating*

For the shortbread
4¹/₂ oz/9 tablespoons butter
²/₃ cup confectioners' sugar
1 egg
1 teaspoon vanilla extract
9 oz/1²/₃ cups all-purpose flour
¹/₄ cup semolina
1 teaspoon baking powder
Pinch of salt
12 unblanched almonds

For the syrup
¹/₂ cup granulated sugar
¹/₃ cup water
Juice of ¹/₂ lemon
1 teaspoon rose water

Equipment
Baking tray

Prep time: 15 minutes
Baking time: 25 minutes
Soaking time: 10 minutes

For the shortbread
Preheat the oven to 350°F and line the baking tray with baking paper.

Beat the butter, confectioners' sugar, egg and vanilla extract together until soft (see figure 1), then sift in the flour, semolina, baking powder and salt and mix to form a soft dough. Roll into balls and place on the baking tray (see figure 2). Press an almond into each one and bake for 25 minutes (see figure 3).

For the syrup
While the shortbread is baking, put all the syrup ingredients into a saucepan and bring to the boil, then turn down the heat and simmer for 5 minutes.

As soon as the shortbread is baked, pour three spoonfuls of syrup onto each one and then let the syrup drain away (see figure 4). You can eat the shortbread straight away or store it in an airtight container for a few days.

1. Beat the butter, confectioners' sugar, egg and vanilla extract together until soft

2. Roll the dough into balls

3. Press and almond into each cookie

4. Pour three spoonfuls of syrup over each cookie and allow the syrup to drain away

ALFAJORES WITH DULCE DE LECHE

Popular in South America, alfajores consist of two layers of thin sweet pastry filled with dulce de leche. I also rolled mine in coconut to finish them off. They taste really good, and because of the amount of butter they have a crumbly texture similar to shortbread.

Alfajores with dulce de leche

Makes 15 pastries   Difficulty rating 🥄

For the pastry
9 oz/1²/₃ cups all-purpose flour
9 oz/18 tablespoons butter
¹/₄ cup confectioners' sugar, plus
    extra for sprinkling
1 teaspoon salt

To assemble
1 (14 oz) can of dulce de leche
    (such as Carnation Caramel);
    see page 120 if you want to
    make your own
¹/₄ teaspoon ground cinnamon
¹/₄ teaspoon ground cloves
¹/₄ teaspoon ground nutmeg
Shredded coconut, for rolling
    (optional)

Equipment
Food processor
2 baking trays
Rolling pin
3¹/₄ in round cookie cutter

Prep time: Pastry 10 minutes, plus 1–2 hours chilling;
filling 5 minutes
Baking time: 10–12 minutes
Assembly time: 10 minutes

For the pastry
Put the pastry ingredients into a food processor and pulse
until combined into a smooth dough. Wrap in plastic wrap and
refrigerate for 1–2 hours.

Preheat the oven to 350°F and line the baking trays with baking
paper.

Flour your work surface and roll out the dough (see figure 1).
As in figure 2, cut out 3¹/₄ inch diameter circles (you should get
about 30 of them), place on a baking tray and refrigerate while
the oven heats up. Bake for 10–12 minutes, then allow to cool.

To assemble
Sprinkle the pastry circles with confectioners' sugar (see figure
3). Mix the dulce de leche with the spices and spread some on
top of half the pastries. Sandwich another pastry on top of the
filling. Roll in coconut if you like (see figure 4).

1. Flour your worktop and roll out the dough

2. Cut out circles of dough

3. Sprinkle the pastry with confectioners' sugar

4. Spread the dulce de leche over half of the pastry circles, sandwich another pastry on top and, if you like, roll the edge of each alfajore in coconut

113

ALMOND ORANGE CAKES

To give these little cakes a beautiful finish, I decided to cover them with almonds, but first I cut out the center of each cake and filled them with sweet mascarpone. The sponge cake is flavored with orange and almonds.

Almond orange cakes

Makes 6 cakes   Difficulty rating ✐

For the cakes
4¹/₂ oz/9 tablespoons butter
¹/₂ cup superfine sugar
2 eggs
Finely grated zest of ¹/₂ orange
   plus a little juice
1 teaspoon almond extract
2³/₄ oz/¹/₂ cup all-purpose flour
¹/₃ cup almond meal
1 teaspoon baking powder

For the icing
6¹/₂ oz/³/₄ cup mascarpone
   cheese
³/₄ cup confectioners' sugar
1 cup sliced blanched almonds,
   to decorate

Equipment
6 dariole cake molds
Apple corer

Prep time: 10 minutes
Cooking time: 25 minutes
Decorating time: 30 minutes

For the cakes
Preheat the oven to 350°F. Grease the dariole or similar cake molds and line the bottom with baking paper.

Cream the butter and superfine sugar together in a bowl until pale and creamy. Beat in the eggs one at a time, then stir in the orange zest, juice and almond extract. Sift in the flour, almond meal and baking powder and fold into the mixture.

Spoon the batter into the molds, about three-quarters full, bake for 25 minutes and then allow to cool.

For the icing
Mix the mascarpone and confectioners' sugar together until smooth (see figure 1). Trim off the top of the sponge cakes. Using the apple corer, remove the center from each cake and set aside (see figure 2). Put a spoonful of mascarpone icing into each cake (see figure 3) and then push the trimmed piece of sponge cake back in place.

Spread more mascarpone icing onto the outside of the sponge cake and decorate with flaked almonds (see figure 4).

1. Mix the confectioners' sugar and mascarpone until smooth and creamy

2. Using an apple corer, remove the center from each cake and set aside

3. Put a spoonful of mascarpone icing into each cake

4. Spread more icing on the outside and decorate with sliced almonds

PRETZEL CARAMEL BARS

❦

These bars are so easy to make and taste amazing.
They consist of a base layer of peanuts, biscuit crumbs and
pretzels, with a salted caramel layer on top. They don't last
very long in my home because everyone loves them.
For speed I used ready-made dulce de leche,
but if you have time they are even better with
homemade caramel.

Pretzel caramel bars

Makes 12 bars   Difficulty rating 🥄

For the base
1/3 cup peanuts
53/4 oz/1 cup pretzels
8 single graham crackers
1/4 cup superfine sugar
31/4 oz/61/2 tablespoons butter
3 heaping tablespoons
   peanut butter

For the topping
1 (14 oz) can of sweetened
   condensed milk or ready-made
   dulce de leche (such
   as Carnation Caramel)
Sea salt for sprinkling
12 pretzels, to decorate

Equipment
8 x 12 in baking tin

Prep time: 10 minutes, but more if making your own dulce de leche
Baking time: 10 minutes
Assembly time: 10 minutes
Setting time: 2 hours

For the base
Preheat the oven to 350°F and line the baking tin with baking paper.

To make the base layer, put the peanuts, pretzels and graham crackers into a food processor and pulse until chopped. Add the sugar. Melt the butter, add it to the bowl with the peanut butter and mix into the chopped mixture.

Press the mixture into the baking tin (see figure 1), bake in the center of the oven for 10 minutes and then allow to cool.

For the topping
To make your own dulce de leche, pour a tin of condensed milk into a sterilized jar, screw on the lid and place in a slow cooker. Cover with water at a boil for 8 hours. Alternatively, preheat the oven to 400°F. Pour the condensed milk into a glass or ceramic ovenproof dish and place this into a larger baking tray (metal is fine). Fill the tray with boiling water to about halfway up the glass dish. Bake for 1 hour 40 minutes. Once cool, whisk the mixture and it is ready to use.

Spread dulce de leche over the top of the base layer (see figure 3) and sprinkle with sea salt. Place whole pretzels evenly on top (see figure 4), allow the dulce de leche to set, then slice and enjoy.

1. Press the pretzel mixture in a baking tray

2. Prepare the dulce de leche

3. Pour the prepared dulce de leche on the baked and cooled pretzel bar base

4. Place whole pretzels evenly on top to decorate

Flower lollipops

Makes 10 lollipops   *Difficulty rating* 🥄

Selection of edible flowers, such
    as violets or primroses
1/3 cup corn syrup
1 cup superfine sugar
1 teaspoon mint extract
1/2 cup water

Equipment
Baking tray
Pastry brush
Candy thermometer
10 lollipop sticks

Prep time: 10 minutes
Cooking time: 10 minutes
Cooling time: 10 minutes

Grease the baking tray or line it with baking paper. Prepare the edible flowers by removing the stalks. Carefully wash them and allow to dry. Fill a bowl with cold water for cooling down the saucepan later.

Heat the remaining ingredients in a saucepan, stirring until the sugar has dissolved. Use a pastry brush dipped in cold water to wash any sugar crystals from the side of the pan down into the syrup. Attach a sugar thermometer to the pan and heat without stirring until the temperature reaches 285°F.

Once it has reached temperature, immediately remove from the heat and place the base of the pan in the bowl of cold water until the temperature lowers to 265°F.

Spoon a circle of the syrup onto the baking tray. Place a lollipop stick and a flower onto each circle, then spoon another circle of syrup on top. Allow to harden.

CANDY-STRIPED MERINGUES

These meringues are cute for winter as they look like candy canes. I use a method that makes the mixture super thick and glossy, and bake them so that they are still soft in the middle — I think they taste better like that. The recipe is easy to remember: weigh the egg whites and use double the quantity of sugar.

Candy-striped meringues

Makes 30 meringues   Difficulty rating ✒

1¹/₃ cup superfine sugar
5 oz egg white (about
    3 egg whites)
Red food coloring

Equipment
Stand mixer fitted with the
    balloon whisk attachment
Piping bag
Glass tumbler
Paintbrush
Baking tray

Prep time: 15 minutes
Baking time: 40 minutes

Preheat the oven to 350°F. Line the baking tray with baking paper and spread the sugar over it. Put the baking tray in the oven to heat up the sugar.

Put the egg whites into the bowl of the stand mixer with the balloon whisk attachment and whisk until the whites become opaque and start to form stiff peaks (see figure 2). When the edges of the sugar turn golden (after about 5 minutes), remove from the oven and turn the temperature down to 200°F.

Add the warm sugar to the egg whites a spoonful at a time and whisk on a high speed for about 10 minutes until the mixture becomes thick and shiny.

Suspend a piping bag inside a tall glass tumbler or similar, turning the bag inside out over the rim of the glass. As in figure 3, use the paintbrush to paint lines of food coloring inside the piping bag (I used gel food coloring and mixed it with a drop of water first). Carefully spoon the meringue mixture into the bag and remove from the glass.

Pipe small mounds of meringue onto the baking tray (see figure 4). Bake for 40 minutes until they can be removed with their bases intact and then allow to cool.

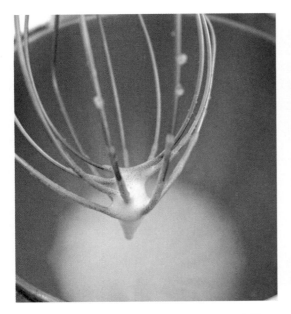

1. Put the egg white into a mixer with a balloon whisk attachment

2. The egg whites are ready when they form stiff peaks

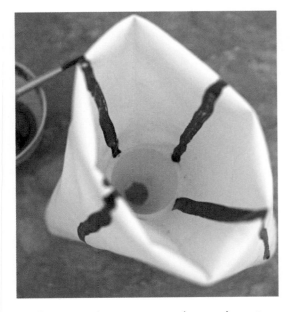

3. Paint four lines of food coloring along the piping bag to make the candy stripe

4. Pipe small mounds of meringue onto the baking tray

CHOCOLATE QUAIL EGGS

I thought it would be fun to make some chocolate eggs that looked like quail eggs. I bought a small plastic egg mold and used a mixture of dark and white chocolate to make them. They would be great for Easter.

Chocolate quail eggs

Makes 15 eggs   Difficulty rating 🥄

2 oz dark or milk chocolate,
  chopped
8 oz white chocolate, chopped
Unsweetened cocoa powder,
  for dusting (optional)

Equipment
Egg mold
Paintbrush

Prep time: 10 minutes
Setting time: 30 minutes

Melt the dark or milk chocolate in a microwave or in a heatproof bowl over a pan of boiling water. Using the paintbrush, paint dots and smudges of chocolate into the egg mold cavities to resemble the speckled shell of a quail's egg (see figure 1). Allow to harden.

Melt the white chocolate. To make solid eggs, fill each mold cavity and refrigerate until the chocolate has hardened (see figure 2). To make hollow eggs, pour the chocolate into the cavities until full, then tip the chocolate back out and lay on a flat surface to harden (see figure 3).

When the chocolate has set, push the egg halves out of the mold and use more melted white chocolate to stick the egg halves together (see figure 4). Dust some of the eggs with cocoa powder to make them look a little darker if you wish.

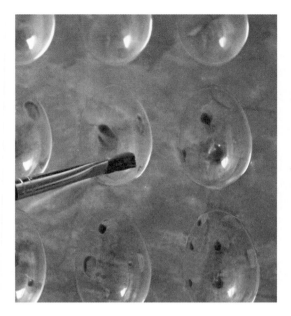

1. Using a paintbrush, paint smudges of chocolate into the egg cavities to resemble a speckled quail's egg

2. Fill each mold with white chocolate. You can make either solid or hollow eggs

3. If making hollow eggs, tip the chocolate back out and lay the mold on a flat surface to harden

4. Use more melted chocolate to stick the egg halves together

Brazilian brigadeiros

Makes 25 truffles   *Difficulty rating* 🖊

Prep time: 10 minutes, plus 10–20 minutes chilling
Assembly time: 20 minutes

For the truffles
1 (14 oz) can sweetened
  condensed milk
2 tablespoons butter
3 tablespoons unsweetened
  cocoa powder

For the coating
Unsweetened cocoa powder,
  desiccated coconut, chopped
  nuts, confectioners' sugar,
  sprinkles, or other decoration
  of your choice

Equipment
Baking tray

For the truffles
Grease the baking tray.

Heat all the truffle ingredients together in a saucepan, stirring until the butter has melted. Continue stirring for about 10 minutes until the mixture thickens. Pour onto the baking tray and refrigerate for 10–20 minutes.

Grease your hands and roll the chilled mixture into small balls. The mixture should be stringy when pulled apart and hold its shape when rolled.

For the coating
Roll the balls in cocoa powder, desiccated coconut, chopped nuts or confectioners' sugar. Add sprinkles or any other decoration of your choice.

STRAWBERRY MARSHMALLOWS

These marshmallows are made with fresh strawberries and taste just like a strawberry milkshake. Other summer berries can be used instead if you prefer. I really enjoy making my own marshmallows. Although they can seem fiddly, the effort is worth it, as they taste so good.

Strawberry marshmallows

Makes 16 large squares   *Difficulty rating* 🥄🥄

2 cups chopped strawberries
1 1/2 tablespoons lemon juice
1 2/3 cups superfine sugar
6 sheets of leaf gelatin
2 egg whites
1/2 teaspoon salt
1 teaspoon vanilla extract
Cconfectioners' sugar and
    cornstarch, for dusting and
    coating

Equipment
Food processor
Stand mixer fitted with balloon
    whisk attachment
Pastry brush
Candy thermometer
8 x 12 in baking tin

Prep time: 30 minutes
Resting time: 4 hours

Put the fruit, lemon juice and 1 tablespoon of superfine sugar into a saucepan and bring to a boil over a low heat until the fruit breaks down. Purée in a food processor and then press through a sieve. Heat for another 10 minutes until the purée has a jam-like consistency (see figure 1). Set aside.

Put the leaf gelatine (if using) into a bowl, cover with water and set aside (see figure 2).

Put the egg whites, salt and 1 tablespoon of superfine sugar into the bowl of the stand mixer fitted with the balloon whisk attachment, but don't turn on the machine yet.

Heat the remaining superfine sugar and 3 tablespoons of water in a heavy-based saucepan, stirring until the sugar has dissolved. Use a pastry brush dipped in cold water to wash any sugar crystals from the side of the pan down into the syrup (see figure 3). Attach a candy thermometer to the pan. When the syrup reaches 248°F, turn on the mixer and whisk the egg whites until stiff peaks start to form (see figure 4).

At the same time, reheat the fruit purée.

1. Heat the strawberry purée until it has a jam-like consistency

2. Soak the leaf gelatine in a bowl of water and set aside

3. When making the syrup, use a pastry brush dipped in cold water to wash sugar crystals from the side of the pan

4. Turn on the mixer and whisk the egg whites once the syrup has reached 248°F

Squeeze out the leaf gelatine (see figure 5), add it to the syrup and stir. The syrup will bubble up, so be careful not to burn yourself. When the syrup reaches 265°F, pour it into the egg whites in a slow stream while whisking at high speed.

Continue for 3 minutes until the mixture is thick and glossy, then add the fruit purée and mix for another 5–8 minutes (see figure 6).

Lightly grease the baking tin. Mix some confectioners' sugar and cornstarch together (equal quantities) and sift over the tin, then tip out any excess (see figure 7). Pour the marshmallow mixture into the tin, spread it out and sift more confectioners' sugar /cornstarch over the top (see figure 8). Leave for 4 hours, then slice and roll the pieces in more confectioners' sugar/ cornstarch. The marshmallows will keep in an airtight container for up to 4 days.

5. Squeeze out the leaf gelatine before adding it to the syrup

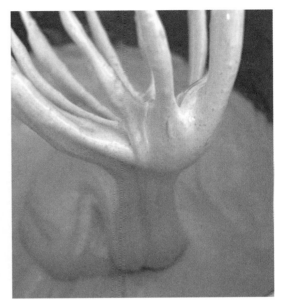

6. Once the mixture is thick and glossy, mix in the fruit purée for another 5-8 minutes

7. Sift a mixture of sugar and cornstarch over a baking tin to coat it, tipping out any excess

8. Spread the marshmallow mixture into the prepared tin

Pistachio and cranberry nougat

Makes 16 pieces   Difficulty rating 🥄🥄

2 sheets of edible rice paper
3 egg whites
1³/₄ cups superfine sugar
¹/₄ cup water
1¹/₂ tablespoons honey
3 teaspoons corn syrup or honey
¹/₂ cup pistachio kernels
¹/₃ cup dried cranberries

Equipment
Stand mixer fitted with the
   balloon whisk attachment
Pastry brush
Candy thermometer
8 x 12 in baking tin

Prep time: 20 minutes
Resting time: 12 hours

Grease the baking tin and line with a sheet of rice paper.

Put the egg whites into the bowl of the stand mixer fitted with the balloon whisk attachment, but don't turn on the machine yet. Heat the sugar, water, honey and corn syrup in a saucepan, stirring until the sugar has dissolved. Use a pastry brush dipped in cold water to wash any sugar crystals from the sides of the pan down into the syrup. Attach a sugar thermometer to the pan and continue heating without stirring. When the syrup reaches 212°F, turn on the mixer and whisk the egg whites until stiff peaks start to form.

When the syrup reaches 248°F, pour it into the egg whites in a slow steady stream while whisking at high speed. Continue for 4–6 minutes until the mixture is thick and glossy.

Spread the mixture into the baking tin and smooth with a hot spatula. Sprinkle nuts and cranberries on top, then cover with another sheet of rice paper. Allow to harden overnight, then slice and enjoy.

CHOCOLATE CHIP COOKIE DOUGH FUDGE

I had a carton of cream that I needed to use up so I decided to make fudge, but for an extra treat I also made some cookie dough and dotted it into the fudge — really tasty and perfect to share with friends.

Chocolate chip cookie dough fudge

Makes 20 small pieces   Difficulty rating 🥄🥄

For the cookie dough

3¼ oz/6½ tablespoons butter
⅓ cup light brown sugar, firmly
   packed
1 teaspoon vanilla extract
3 teaspoons corn syrup or honey
5½ oz/1 cup all-purpose flour
⅓ cup chocolate chips

For the fudge

½ cup whole milk
½ cup heavy whipping cream
1¼ cups superfine sugar
½ cup light brown sugar, lightly
   packed
3¼ oz/6½ tablespoons butter
Pinch of salt

Equipment

Baking tray
8 x 12 in baking tin
Candy thermometer

Prep time: cookie dough 10 minutes; fudge 5 minutes
Cooking time: 20 minutes
Assembly time: 10 minutes

For the cookie dough

To make the cookie dough, cream the butter and sugar together in a bowl until pale and creamy. Stir in the vanilla extract and corn syrup or honey, then sift in the flour, add the chocolate chips and mix into a dough. Roll into small balls (see figure 1) and place on a baking tray in the freezer for about 30 minutes to firm up.

For the fudge

Line the baking tin with baking paper.

Heat the milk, cream, both sugars and butter in a heavy-based saucepan, stirring until the sugar has dissolved and the butter has melted. Attach a sugar thermometer to the pan and bring the mixture to a boil (see figure 2). When the temperature reaches 245°F, remove from the heat and stir in the salt.

Allow the mixture to cool slightly and then stir again until the shine starts to disappear. Pour into the cake tin and allow to cool (see figure 3).

Press the cookie dough balls into the fudge (see figure 4) and then slice. Keep in a cool, dry place in an airtight container for 1 week.

1. Roll the cookie dough into small balls

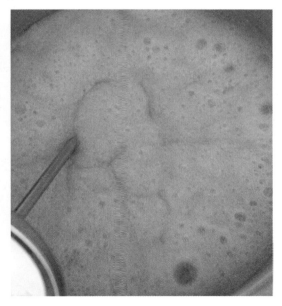

2. While making the fudge, attach a sugar thermometer and remove from heat when the temperature reaches 245°F

3. Pour the fudge into a cake tin and allow to cool

4. Press the cookie dough balls into the fudge

4. Party treats

Cheesecake-stuffed tulips

Makes 8 stuffed tulips   Difficulty rating 🥄

8 whole tulips and 5 tulip petals
1 cup graham cracker crumbs
1¹/₂ tablespoons granulated
  sugar
¹/₄ cup heavy whipping cream
¹/₃ cup cream cheese
1 cup confectioners' sugar
1¹/₂ tablespoons lemon juice
Pink or purple food coloring

Equipment
Piping bag

Prep time: 10 minutes
Assembly time: 8–10 minutes

Prepare the tulip flowers by cutting out the centers so that you are left with just the petals held together by a small amount of stalk. Carefully wash them to remove any pollen, then allow to dry. Chop the five tulip petals.

Mix the biscuit crumbs with the granulated sugar and spoon some into each flower.

Whip the cream to stiff peaks (it may be easier to whip more cream than you need and keep whatever is left over for another dish). Mix the whipped cream with the cream cheese, confectioners' sugar, lemon juice and chopped petals. Stir in some food coloring, adding a small amount at a time until you achieve a color you like.

Spoon the mixture into a piping bag and pipe some into each flower. You can eat the whole thing, leaving just the stalk, or serve with small spoons and use the tulips as bowls.

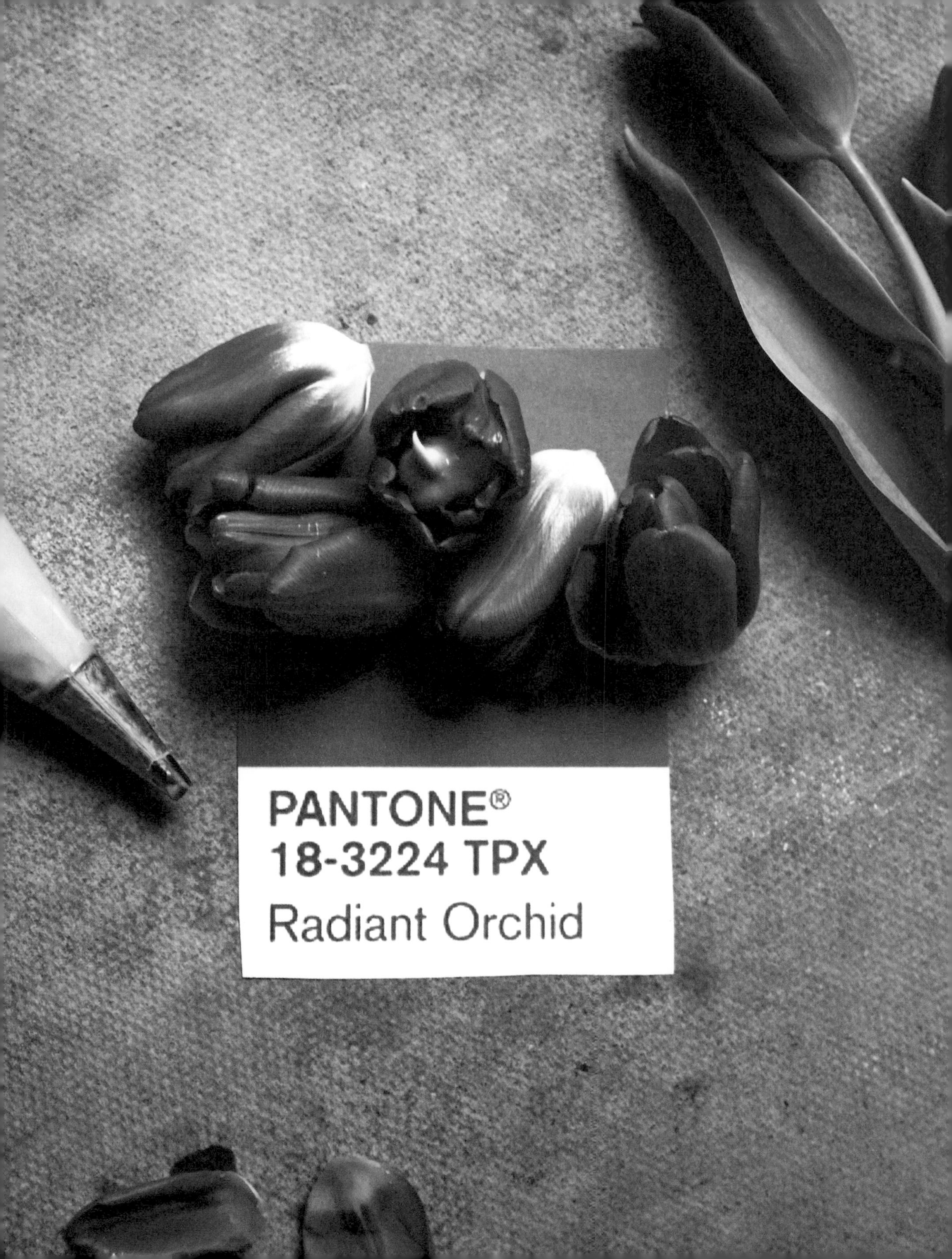

PANTONE®
18-3224 TPX
Radiant Orchid

HOME-MADE POP TARTS

These little pies are so easy to make and they taste delicious. I filled them with peaches and blueberries but you can use any other fruit that you happen to have at home.

Home-made pop tarts

Makes 6 tarts   Difficulty rating 🥄

For the pastry
7 oz/1¹/₃ cups all-purpose flour
4¹/₂ ounces/9 tablespoons butter
1¹/₂ tablespoons superfine sugar
1 egg yolk

For the filling
5 small white peaches
³/₄ cup blueberries
¹/₄ cup superfine sugar

For the icing
¹/₂ cup confectioners' sugar

Equipment
Rolling pin
Baking tray
Pastry wheel (optional)

Prep time: 30 minutes
Baking time: 20 minutes
Decorating time: 5 minutes

For the pastry
Put the flour, butter and sugar into a food processor and pulse to combine. Add the egg yolk and mix to form a dough. Cover with plastic wrap and refrigerate for 20 minutes.

Preheat the oven to 350°F.

For the filling
To make the filling, peel the peaches, remove the stones and cut into slices. Put all of the peach slices and half the blueberries into a bowl and sprinkle with half the sugar. Put the remaining blueberries into a saucepan with the rest of the sugar and boil for a few minutes until the liquid reduces. Press through a sieve to get a smooth syrup, and reserve the saucepan (don't wash it just yet).

Roll out the dough and cut into 12 rectangles (see figure 1). Spoon some syrup and then some of the fruit mixture onto half of the rectangles (see figure 2). Place another pastry rectangle on top, press together around the edges and cut a small slit in the top. Use a pastry wheel to flute the edges of the tarts if you wish (see figure 3). Carefully place each pastry onto a baking tray lined with baking paper. Bake for 20 minutes.

For the icing
Put the confectioners' sugar into the pan that the blueberry syrup was cooked in and mix to make a thick icing, adding a little water if necessary. Drizzle the icing over the tarts (see figure 4).

1. Cut the dough into twelve equal rectangles

2. Place the filling on half of the rectangles

3. Place another pastry rectangle on top, seal around the edges and trim

4. Drizzle the icing over the tarts

CHURROS WITH CINNAMON SUGAR AND DULCE DE LECHE

I love churros, but I decided to change their shape and roll the dough into balls rather than make long piped churros. The dough is basically like a choux pastry that is fried, and it is firm enough to roll in your hands. I found that having slightly damp hands made rolling easier. Traditionally churros are eaten with a chocolate dipping sauce, but I have used dulce de leche instead.

Churros with cinnamon sugar and dulce de leche

Makes 16 churros   *Difficulty rating* 🖊

Prep time: 10 minutes
Cooking time: 20 minutes

For the coating
½ cup superfine sugar
1 teaspoon ground cinnamon

For the churros
2 eggs
3¼ oz/6½ tablespoons butter
2¼ tablespoons brown sugar
Pinch of salt
1 cup water
5½ oz/1 cup all-purpose flour
½ teaspoon vanilla extract
Sunflower oil, for deep frying

To serve
1 (14 oz) can dulce de leche
(such as Carnation Caramel);
see page 120 if you want to
make your own

Equipment
Stand mixer
Piping bag (optional)
Deep fryer (optional)

For the coating
Mix the sugar and cinnamon together in a bowl for coating the churros, once cooked, and set aside.

For the churros
Beat the eggs in a bowl. Put the butter, sugar, salt and water into a saucepan and bring to a boil, stirring until the butter has melted. Take the pan off the heat, add the flour and beat in using a wooden spoon until the mixture forms a smooth paste that pulls away from the sides of the pan. Return to the heat, stirring constantly, for another minute. Transfer the pastry mixture to the bowl of a stand mixer (see figure 1) and start mixing, slowing adding the eggs until combined. Add the vanilla extract.

Either roll small balls of the mixture with your hands (see figure 2) or use a piping bag to pipe them. Heat the sunflower oil in a pan or deep fryer until it reaches 150°F. You can test the temperature by sticking a wooden spoon into the oil. If the oil starts to bubble around the wooden spoon, it's ready. Drop a few of the churro balls into the oil and cook on each side for 2–3 minutes (see figure 3), then roll in the cinnamon coating (see figure 4).

To serve
Spoon the dulce de leche into a bowl and serve as a dipping sauce for the churros.

1. Transfer the pastry to a stand mixer and mix, slowly adding the eggs until combined

2. Roll small balls of the dough

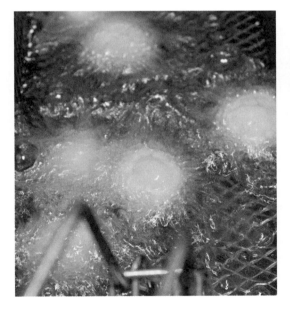

3. Drop a few churro balls at a time into a deep-fryer and cook on each side for 2–3 minutes until golden

4. Roll the churro balls in the cinnamon sugar mixture

CHOCOLATE FRUIT AND NUT SALAMI

This is one of the most amazing things I have ever tried. It is so easy to make and is a great Christmas gift idea. The recipe will make either one large salami or two smaller ones, which is what I decided to do. It may look like a salami but it tastes like a cross between ganache and rocky road just like a fridge cake.

Chocolate fruit and nut salami

Makes 1 large or 2 small salamis   Difficulty rating 🥄

9 oz dark chocolate, chopped
3^1/$_4$ oz/6^1/$_2$ tablespoons butter
^{3}/$_4$ cup superfine sugar
3 eggs
1^1/$_2$ tablespoons unsweetened
   cocoa powder
1^1/$_2$ tablespoons vanilla extract
8–10 Amaretti or equivalent
   amount graham crackers
^{1}/$_3$ cup pistachio kernels
^{1}/$_3$ cup sliced blanched almonds
4 tablespoons hazelnuts
4 tablespoons dried cranberries
Confectioners' sugar, for coating

Equipment
Plastic wrap
Cheesecloth and baker's
   twine (optional)

Prep time: 30 minutes
Resting time: 12 hours

Melt the chocolate in a microwave or in a heatproof bowl over a pan of boiling water, then set aside.

Cream the butter and sugar together in a bowl until pale and creamy, then beat in the eggs one at a time. (If you are worried about eating uncooked eggs, whisk them in a bowl over a pan of boiling water until they have thickened, then add them to the mixture.)

Stir the cocoa into the melted chocolate, add this to the butter and egg mixture and combine well. Stir in the vanilla extract.

Break the biscuits into chunks and add to the mixture with the nuts and cranberries. Stir together and then refrigerate for 30 minutes.

Following figures 1 and 2, lay a piece of plastic wrap over your worktop, place some of the chilled mixture on top and use the plastic wrap to roll it into a salami shape. Twist the ends of the plastic wrap (figure 3) and refrigerate overnight.

Unwrap the salami and rub on some confectioners' sugar (figure 4). To make it look like a real salami, wrap it in a piece of cheesecloth (muslin) and use baker's twine to tie it up.

1. Lay out a piece of plastic wrap. You can dust it lightly with confectioners' sugar

2. Place some of the chilled mixture onto the plastic wrap and use the plastic wrap to roll it into a salami shape

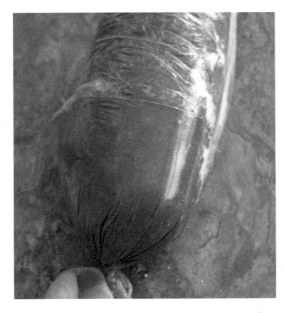

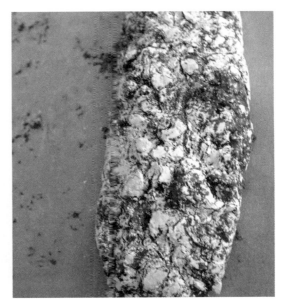

3. Twist the ends of the plastic wrap to seal it

4. Once chilled overnight, rub the fruit and nut salami with confectioners' sugar

SUMMER CHERRY PIE S'MORES

❧

I decided to put a summer spin on the traditional s'mores and make homemade cherry marshmallows and lattice cookies rather than graham crackers or digestive biscuits. They taste wonderful and I really enjoy making my own marshmallows.

Summer cherry pie s'mores

Makes 16 large marshmallows and 12 lattice cookies   *Difficulty rating* 🥄🥄

For the marshmallows

12 oz/2^1/$_3$ cups pitted cherries

1^1/$_2$ tablespoons lemon juice

1^2/$_3$ cups superfine sugar

6 sheets of leaf gelatine or
   3^1/$_2$ sachets of unflavored
   powdered gelatine

2 egg whites

^{1}/$_2$ teaspoon salt

1 teaspoon vanilla extract

Confectioners' sugar and
   cornstarch, for dusting
   and coating

For the lattice cookies

7 oz/1^1/$_3$ cups all-purpose flour

^{1}/$_2$ cup superfine sugar

4^1/$_2$ oz/9 tablespoons butter

1 teaspoon vanilla extract

1 egg

Equipment

Food processor

Stand mixer fitted with balloon
   whisk attachment

8 x 12 in baking tin

Baking tray

Rolling pin

Prep time: marshmallows 30 minutes; cookies 20 minutes
Resting/chilling time: marshmallows 4 hours;
cookies 30 minutes
Baking time: 6–8 minutes

For the marshmallows

Make the cherry marshmallows using the method described on pages 136–38, reserving a little of the cherry purée for serving.

For the lattice cookies

Put all the ingredients for the cookies into the food processor and mix until combined. Tip out onto your worktop and roll into a ball, then cover with plastic wrap and refrigerate for 30 minutes.

Preheat the oven to 350°F and line the baking tray with baking paper.

Roll out the cookie dough and cut into strips, then lattice them together by weaving the strips over and under each other (see figures 1, 2 and 3). Cut into equal-sized cookies (see figure 4), place on the baking tray and bake for 6–8 minutes.

To serve, sandwich pieces of marshmallow between two lattice cookies with a little cherry purée.

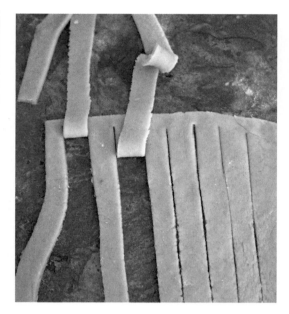

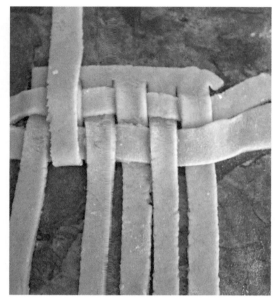

1. To make a lattice, first lift every other strip and lay it above the sheet of dough

2. Weave separate strips of dough over and under the strips of the sheet of dough

3. Continue until you have a full lattice

4. Trim each lattice cookie

Buckwheat cake with berry compote

Serves 8 to 10   Difficulty rating 🥄

For the sponge
9 oz/18 tablespoons butter
1 cup superfine sugar
4 eggs
1 teaspoon vanilla extract
7³/₄ oz/1²/₃ cups buckwheat flour
2 teaspoons baking powder
2 tablespoons milk

For the berry compote
10 blackberries
10 raspberries
5 strawberries, chopped
¹/₄ cup of sugar
1 tablespoon water

To decorate
³/₄ cup whipping cream
1¹/₂ tablespoons confectioners'
   sugar, plus extra for dusting
Fresh berries, to decorate
Fresh flowers, to decorate

Equipment
4¹/₂ in round cake tins

Prep time: 10 minutes
Freezing time: 25–30 minutes
Decorating time: 10 minutes

For the sponge
Preheat the oven to 350°F, and grease the two cake tins.

In a mixing bowl beat the butter and sugar until pale and creamy. Then add the eggs one at a time, making sure each one is properly combined before adding the next. Add 1 teaspoon vanilla extract, sift in the flour and baking powder and fold into the mixture. Add the milk to loosen the batter a little.

Split the mixture equally between the two tins. Put the tins in the oven and bake on the same shelf for approximately 25–30 minutes. Allow to cool completely.

For the berry compote
Heat all the ingredients over a medium heat until the berries have broken down and the liquid has reduced a little (the consistency should be like jam), approximately 10 minutes. Allow to cool.

To decorate
Whisk the whipping cream with the sugar until the cream forms stiff peaks. Place the bottom layer of your cake on to your chosen cake stand or plate. Spread half of the whipped cream over the bottom layer, and then spread on the cooled compote. Place the next layer of sponge cake on top, and spread over the rest of the cream. Decorate with berries and any flowers (I added a rose), and finally dust with confectioners' sugar.

Pineapple passion fruit sorbet

Makes 2 cups sorbet   Difficulty rating

1 pineapple
1 cup water
1/4 cup superfine sugar
3 teaspoons honey
3 passion fruit

Equipment
Blender

Prep time: 10 minutes
Freezing time: 3 hours

Scoop out the soft part of the pineapple and discard the hard center. Put the pineapple flesh into the blender and purée. Pour the purée into a saucepan and add the water, sugar and honey. Scoop the seeds out of the passion fruit and add to the pan. Stir over a medium heat until the sugar has dissolved.

Pour the sorbet mixture into the pineapple shell and freeze for 30 minutes. Remove the pineapple from the freezer, stir the sorbet and then freeze for another 30 minutes. Stir the sorbet once again and then freeze for another 2 hours or until needed.

BAKEWELL TART ICE CREAM

Bakewell tart is my partner's favourite sweet treat, so with this recipe I have tried to replicate it as an ice cream flavor. I also made some mini Bakewell tarts to serve on top.

Bakewell tart ice cream

Makes 4 cups ice cream and 8 mini tarts   Difficulty rating   🥄🥄

For the ice cream
1 1/3 cups whipping cream
1 cup milk
1 vanilla pod
2 teaspoons almond extract
3/4 cup superfine sugar
6 egg yolks
4 tablespoons raspberry jam
5 tablespoons flaked almonds

For the pastry and filling
3 1/2 oz/2/3 cup all-purpose flour
1/4 cup superfine sugar
   plus 3 teaspoons
Pinch of salt
3 tablespoons ice-cold water
2 drops of almond extract
2 1/4 oz/4 1/2 tablespoons butter
1 egg
1 3/4 oz/1/3 cup self-rising flour
3 tablespoons almond meal
3 tablespoons raspberry jam
Sliced blanched almonds

Equipment
Ice-cream maker
Food processor
Rolling pin
Mini muffin tin and baking beans

Prep time: ice cream: 30 minutes, plus churning time;
tarts: 20 minutes
Freezing/chilling time: ice cream: 3 hours; pastry: 20 minutes
Baking time: 18–20 minutes or longer

For the ice cream
Put the cream, milk, vanilla pod and extract into a saucepan. Bring to a slow boil, remove from the heat, cover, and infuse for 10 minutes. Remove the vanilla pod and return to a boil. Mix the sugar and egg yolks in a bowl and pour in a quarter of the infused liquid, whisking constantly, to temper the yolks. Pour the yolks into the saucepan and return to the heat, stirring until the mixture thickens. Pour into an ice-cream maker and churn according to the maker's instructions. Stir in the jam and almonds, then transfer to a 4-cup loaf tin and freeze for about 3 hours.

For the pastry and filling
Mix the all-purpose flour, 3 teaspoons sugar and salt together in the food processor, then add the water and 1 drop of almond extract and pulse until combined. On your work surface, roll the dough into a ball, cover with plastic wrap and refrigerate for 20 minutes.

Preheat the oven to 350°F and grease the mini muffin tin. Roll out the pastry, cut out small circles and press into the cups of the tin. Put baking paper and baking beans into each pastry (see figure 1) and blind bake for 10 minutes. Allow to cool.

Cream the butter and the rest of the sugar together for the filling, then whisk in the egg. Stir in the rest of the almond extract, then sift and fold in the self-rising flour and almond meal. Spoon a layer of jam into the bottom of each tart case, then pipe in the filling (see figures 2 and 3). Sprinkle the top with flaked almonds and bake for 8–10 minutes or longer, depending on the size.

1. Blind bake the tarts using baking paper and baking beans or uncooked rice

2. Spoon a thin layer of jam into the tart case

3. Pipe the almond filling over the jam

4. To serve, you can sprinkle sliced almonds and drizzle raspberry sauce over a scoop of ice cream and crown with a mini tart

PEACH AND BLUEBERRY FROZEN YOGURT CAKE

This is easy to make, and is lovely and refreshing on a warm summer day. I used peaches and blueberries, but other fruits like strawberries and raspberries would also work. I used a jelly mold to make this cake but you can use any shape of cake mold that you like.

Peach and blueberry frozen yogurt cake

Makes a 4-cup cake   Difficulty rating

Prep time: 20 minutes
Freezing time: 4 hours

For the cake
1 1/2 cups blueberries
1/2 cup superfine sugar
4 peaches
1 cup whipping cream
24 fl oz/2 3/4 cups plain yogurt

For the syrup
1/4 cup blueberries, plus extra for
    decorating
2 1/4 tablespoons superfine sugar
1 teaspoon water

Equipment
2 saucepans
Food processor
4-cup cake mold

For the cake
Put the blueberries and half the sugar into one saucepan with 1 tablespoon of water. Put the peaches and remaining sugar into the other pan. Simmer both pans over a low heat until the fruit becomes soft. Peel and chop the peaches, purée them in the food processor and then press through a sieve into a bowl. Press the blueberry mixture through a sieve into another bowl (no need to use a food processor for this one).

In a large bowl, whip the cream and then stir in the yogurt. Add some of the yogurt mixture to the peach purée. Put some more of the yogurt mixture into another bowl and stir in a few tablespoons of the blueberry purée. Mix the remaining yogurt and blueberry mixtures together. (You need to make two shades of blueberry yogurt and one of peach.)

Pour the darkest blueberry yogurt into the mold first and freeze for 5 minutes (see figure 1). Repeat with the lighter blueberry mixture (see figure 2), and finally with the peach mixture. Freeze for about 4 hours. To release the yogurt from its mold, dip the mold in hot water for a few seconds (see figure 3).

For the syrup
Put all of the syrup ingredients into a saucepan and boil for a few minutes until the liquid reduces. Press through a sieve to get a smooth syrup. Drizzle the syrup over the cake (see figure 4) and decorate with fresh blueberries.

1. First pour the darkest blueberry mixture into the mold and freeze for 5 minutes

2. Pour the lighter blueberry mixture into the mold and freeze for another five minutes

3. After the yogurt has been frozen for 4 hours, release it from its mold by dipping the mold in hot water for a few seconds

4. Drizzle the syrup over the yogurt cake and decorate with fresh blueberries

BERRY ICE CREAM WITH HOMEMADE CONES

It's fun making my own ice cream, especially when there is no need to churn it. This ice cream is made with condensed milk, whipping cream and the juice of blueberries, raspberries and cherries. The cones are easy to make too, and if you don't have a cone mold use a circle of card rolled into a cone shape.

Berry ice cream with homemade cones

Makes 2 cups of ice cream and 5 cones   Difficulty rating

For the ice cream

$^2/_3$ cup raspberries

$^1/_2$ cup blueberries

$^2/_3$ cup pitted cherries

$^1/_4$ cup superfine sugar

$1^1/_2$ tablespoons water

1 cup whipping cream

3 tablespoons confectioners' sugar

1 (14 oz) can sweetened condensed milk

For the cones

3 tablespoons butter, plus extra for frying

$^1/_2$ cup superfine sugar

$2^1/_4$ tablespoons unsweetened cocoa powder

2 eggs

$1^1/_2$ tablespoons milk

1 teaspoon vanilla extract

$1^3/_4$ oz/$^1/_3$ cup all-purpose flour

Butter or oil, for frying

Equipment

Stand mixer

Metal tin

Frying pan

Cone shaper

Prep time: ice cream 20 minutes; cones 10 minutes
Freezing/chilling time: ice cream 4–6 hours; cones 20 minutes
Cooking time: 5 minutes per cone

For the ice cream

Put the fruit, superfine sugar and water into a saucepan and simmer for 10 minutes. Once the fruit has broken down, mash it and then press through a sieve. Allow to cool. Using the stand mixer, whisk the cream and confectioners' sugar together until stiff peaks form. Pour in the condensed milk, add the fruit purée and combine. Pour into a metal tin and freeze for at least 4–6 hours.

For the cones

Melt the butter and then mix together with the sugar and cocoa in a bowl. Add the eggs, milk and vanilla extract and combine until smooth (see figure 1). Mix in the flour and then refrigerate for 20 minutes.

Heat a little butter in a frying pan. Ladle about 3 tablespoons of the cone mixture into the pan (see figure 2), spread it around and cook for a minute. Flip over and cook on the other side for another minute. Repeat to cook for a minute or two more on each side. When the color turns brown, remove from the pan and immediately roll into a cone shape (see figures 3 and 4), trying not to burn your fingers. Allow to cool, then fill with a scoop of ice cream and enjoy.

1. Mix the cocoa mixture, eggs, milk and vanilla extract until smooth

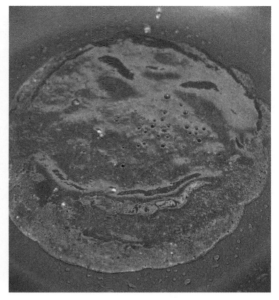

2. Ladle three tablespoons of cone mix onto a hot pan

3. When the cone is browned, quickly remove from pan and use a cone shaper to make a cone

4. Roll the cone around the shaper and allow to cool. Cook and shape the remaining cones in the same way

Kiwi lime popsicles

Makes 6 popsicles   Difficulty rating 🖊

5 kiwi fruit
2 cups water
Juice and grated zest of 1 lime
11 mint leaves
¹/₄ cup superfine sugar

Equipment
Food processor
Lollipop molds
6 lollipop sticks or twigs

Prep time: 10 minutes
Freezing time: 2–4 hours

Peel and chop four of the kiwi fruit and place in a saucepan with the water. Add the lime juice and zest and five of the mint leaves. Stir in the sugar and simmer until it has dissolved.

Remove the mint leaves pour the mixture into the food processor and pulse. Press though a sieve into a jug, then pour into the lollipop molds. Slice the remaining kiwi, push a lollipop stick through the middle of each slice and place one on top of each mold so that the kiwi will be at the base of the popsicle. I used twigs as lollipop sticks; if you want to do the same, make sure they are properly washed.

Add a mint leaf on top of each kiwi slice at the base of the lollipop stick and freeze for 2–4 hours.

CHAMOMILE AND LEMON BAKED ALASKA

I dreamt up this flavor combination and was desperate to see it in action, so I set about breaking in my new cook's blowtorch and making this great dessert. I like the idea of making a baked Alaska with a difference, and the flavors are lovely together: chamomile and honey ice cream on a lemony sponge cake base covered with shiny Italian meringue. I picked flowers from my garden and used them to decorate.

Chamomile and lemon baked Alaska

Serves 6 to 8   Difficulty rating ✔✔

For the ice cream
1¹/₃ cups whipping cream
1 cup milk
1 vanilla pod
2 chamomile tea bags
³/₄ cup superfine sugar
6 egg yolks
2¹/₄ tablespoons honey

For the cake
2¹/₄ oz/4¹/₂ tablespoons butter
¹/₄ cup superfine sugar
1 egg
Zest of 1 lemon
Juice of ¹/₂ lemon
2¹/₂ oz/¹/₂ cup self-rising flour
1 teaspoon baking powder
Pinch of salt
3 teaspoons milk

For the meringue
4 oz egg white (about
   3 egg whites)
1 cup superfine sugar
¹/₃ cup water

To decorate
Fresh flowers, such as chamomile
   or daisies (washed and dried)

Prep time: ice cream 20 minutes, plus churning time;
cake 10 minutes; meringue 20 minutes
Freezing time: 2–4 hours
Baking time: 25 minutes
Decorating time: 10 minutes

For the ice cream
To make the ice cream, put the cream, milk, vanilla pod and tea bags into a saucepan. Bring to a slow boil, then remove from the heat and leave with the lid on for 10 minutes to infuse the flavors. Remove the vanilla pod and tea bags and bring back to the boil. Mix the sugar and egg yolks together in a bowl. Pour a quarter of the infused liquid into the bowl, whisking constantly, to temper the egg yolks. Pour the tempered eggs into the saucepan and return to the heat, stirring until the mixture thickens and coats the back of a spoon.

Pour into an ice-cream maker, add the honey and churn according to the maker's instructions. Transfer to a round, deep container of about the same diameter as your cake tin (I used a jug) and freeze for 2–4 hours. I find lining the container with plastic wrap before pouring in the ice cream is helpful when removing the ice cream from the container after it has frozen.

For the cake
Preheat the oven to 350°F. Grease and line the bottom of the cake tin. Cream the butter and sugar together in a bowl until pale and creamy. Beat in the egg, then stir in the lemon zest and juice. Sift in the flour, baking powder and salt and fold into the mixture. Stir in the milk to loosen the batter a little. Spoon into the cake tin, bake for 20 minutes and then allow to cool.

1. Temper your eggs by pouring a little of the infused liquid and mixing constantly

2. Ensure the container you're freezing your ice cream in and your cake tin are roughly the same diameter

3. When removing the frozen ice cream, dip the container in hot water to help release it

4. Place the set ice cream on top of the cake and return to the freezer

Equipment

Ice-cream maker

Round, deep container, the same
diameter as your cake tin

Round cake tin (the tin I used
was 8 inches in diameter)

Stand mixer fitted with the
balloon whisk attachment

Pastry brush

Candy thermometer

Kitchen blowtorch

Remove the ice cream from its container – I usually dip the container in hot water to help release it (see figure 3). Place the ice cream on top of the cooled sponge cake (see figure 4) and return to the freezer until the meringue is ready.

For the meringue

Put the egg whites into the bowl of the stand mixer fitted with the balloon whisk attachment, but don't turn on the machine yet. Heat the sugar and water in a heavy-based saucepan, stirring until the sugar has dissolved. Use a pastry brush dipped in cold water to wash any sugar crystals from the sides of the pan down into the syrup. Attach a sugar thermometer to the pan. When the syrup reaches 230°F, turn on the mixer and whisk the egg whites until stiff peaks start to form (see figure 5).

When the syrup reaches 248°F, pour it into the egg whites in a slow steady stream while whisking at high speed. Continue for 6–8 minutes until the mixture is thick and glossy. Adding the hot syrup cooks the egg whites, so there is no need for further baking.

To assemble

As in figure 6, spoon the meringue over the ice-cream covered cake (don't be too neat as any ridges and swirls will color nicely) and glaze with a kitchen blowtorch (see figure 7). Press in the flowers to decorate.

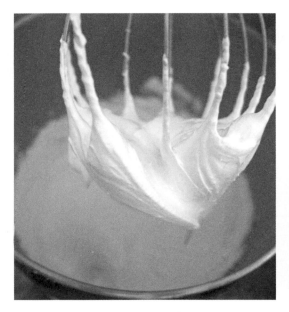

5. Whisk the egg whites until stiff peaks begin to form

6. Cover the cake with meringue

7. Glaze the meringue with a kitchen blowtorch

8. Decorate the cake with the flowers. When you cut open the cake you will see the different layers

ACKNOWLEDGMENTS

I would like to dedicate this book to my nan, Jean, who sadly passed away in May 2014. I would also like to thank Drew Smith for finding my blog and helping me to start this book, and Jan from Maddocks Farm Organics for supplying me with edible flowers.

For more recipes and inspiration, please visit my blog at www.twiggstudios.com

INDEX

Copyright © Elwin Street Productions 2015
Conceived and produced by
Elwin Street Productions
14 Clerkenwell Green
London EC1R 0DP
elwinstreet.com

Photographer: Aimee Twigger

Published in the United States of America by
Gibbs Smith
PO Box 667
Layton, Utah 84041
www.gibbs-smith.com
Orders: 1.800.835.4993

Library of Congress Control Number: 2017932669
ISBN 978-1-4236-4800-0

IMPORTANT: Those who might be at risk from the effects of salmonella poisoning (the elderly,
pregnant women, young children and those suffering from immune deficiency diseases) should consult
their doctor with any concerns about eating raw eggs.

OVEN GUIDE: You may find cooking times vary depending on the oven you are using. For convection
ovens, as a general rule, set the oven temperature to 35°F lower than indicated in the recipe.